# Help Your Baby Build a Healthy Body

# Help Your Baby Build a Healthy Body

## A New Exercise and Massage Program for the First Five Formative Years

## BY TAMARA MEYER

*With an Introduction by Irene Chatoor, M.D.*
*and a Foreword by Lynn A. Balzer-Martin, Ph.D., O.T.R.*

CROWN PUBLISHERS, INC.

NEW YORK

All photography in this book by Joan Marcus

Published by Crown Publishers, Inc.,
One Park Avenue, New York, New York 10016 and
simultaneously in Canada by
General Publishing Company Limited

Manufactured in the United States of America

Library of Congress Cataloging in Publication Data

Meyer, Tamara.

Help your baby build a healthy body.

Includes index.

1. Infants—Care and hygiene.   2. Exercise for children.
3. Massage for children.   4. Parent and child.

I. Title
TJ61.M623   1984        649'.4        83-20926
ISBN 0-517-54924-7
      0-517-54925-5 (pbk)

10 9 8 7 6 5 4 3 2 1

First Edition

Designed by Joanna Nelson

*For my parents,*
*Eric and Ursula Meyer*

# Contents

# Acknowledgments

For their invaluable contributions to this book, I would like to thank Joseph Newman, Joan Marcus, and Anita Diamant. I would like to give special thanks also to Lucia Newman, Dr. Irene Chatoor, Dr. Lynn Balzer-Martin, Warren Rogers, and Mitchell Fagan; also to Karl Dobbratz, who appears in many photographs in this book, to the children—Gregory Vershbow, Charles Danko, Wynter Pradier, Briana M. Gasbarre, Roxanne Duclos, Nicolas Dobbratz, Cary L. Dobkin—and to their parents.

I would also like to thank Lisa Healy, Tim Gallwey, Lani Morrison, Michael Black, Lenn Cooper, Christopher Tubergen, Fletcher Drake, Rachel Weisman, Julie Polinger, Arni Polinger; John, Helen, and Jessica Kronstadt; Elise, Stanley, and Josh Fagan; Dr. and Mrs. Eugene Goldstein, the National Library of Medicine, and the Library of Congress.

# Foreword

Parents who seek to enhance their child's development—physical, social, and emotional—will find this book to be a valuable resource. Tamara Meyer is knowledgeable and skillful in her presentation of massage and exercise techniques. She provides a clear "how-to" approach, combined with factual information to enable the reader to understand the rationale for such a program. Readers will especially appreciate the way in which this book relates massage and exercise to some of the most interesting, up-to-date concepts regarding infant and child development.

The book is comprehensive, making a special effort to address current issues such as parent-infant bonding and the trend toward increased participation by fathers in the birth of the child and in all aspects of care giving. It also deals with the problem of stress, which has popularly been regarded as nonexistent in young children. Increasingly, however, professionals are discovering that the pressures of life in much of our society are felt by children as well as by adults. Building upon such recognition, the author explores the roles of massage and exercise in light of their potential to benefit both parent and child by reducing tension and stress.

A wealth of knowledge that has been accumulated through research in recent years has been incorporated into the growing field of infant stimulation. We now can identify the three basic senses that are the earliest to mature via the development of the nervous system of the fetus while still within the womb. The senses are touch (tactile), balance and movement (vestibular), and body position (kinesthesia or proprioception). Precisely because of their early maturation, these basic senses are especially available to the infant for use in early experiences with the environment. But the need to stimulate these senses systematically is not as obvious to parents as the need to provide varied sights and sounds for their infant and young child. Nevertheless, stimulation of the three early-maturing senses is vital since they are, relatively, the most sophisticated senses that newborns and young children can rely on. Moreover, they are essential for the development of the child's motor skills. Indeed, this concept is also inherent in the fact that psychologist Jean Piaget categorizes the child's entire first stage of learning, from approximately birth to age two years, as the sensorimotor period. I can think of no better way to provide a child with appropriate experiences in the three basic senses than through a structured program of massage and exercise.

Parents will be gratified that this book does not make simplistic assumptions, such as there is only one kind of "typical" family situation. The author is sensitive to addressing the particular needs of premature infants as well as those of full-term babies. She also addresses the needs of an infant who may initially be separated from the parents for some duration due to medical necessity. The particular relevance of her techniques for parents who adopt an infant or young child is also set forth.

Among the many new publications on infant and child development that are appearing with such frequency of late, this book occupies a niche of its own. Parents within varied family structures and with diverse life-styles can readily adapt these massage and exercise techniques to promote fitness and health while nurturing the overall development of their infant and young child.

Lynn A. Balzer-Martin, Ph.D., O.T.R.
Child Development Center
Department of Pediatrics
Georgetown University Medical Center
Washington, D.C.

# Introduction

A baby poses many questions to his or her parents. How do parents get to know this little person and facilitate his development? A mother's wish to love and care for her baby does not necessarily give her the skill to encourage the baby's development. Many young parents find themselves alone and away from the support and guidance of the extended family. Some fathers find it strange and feel uneasy picking up a baby, who appears so fragile. Frequently parents feel uncertain about how much to touch their infant and which exercises might be appropriate at which age.

This book tells you how to learn and enjoy with your baby the development of his motor skills. The exercise and massage program developed by Tamara Meyer is the outgrowth of her work with children and parents over many years, combined with her thorough research of exercise and massage practices in several countries around the world. The book reflects her translation of recent findings in child development and stress management into improving the day-to-day life of parents and their children through exercise and massage. She presents an in-depth discussion of the history and theories of exercise and massage and takes parents step by step through an exercise and massage program from infancy through the first five years of life. The book describes how to go over each muscle group and how to achieve an even balance between working the muscle and relaxing it. The secret is that through the process of exertion the limits of strength are built up in the young body, thus the child becomes more agile and better coordinated.

*Help Your Baby Build a Healthy Body* encourages young parents to grow with their infant, to find ways of touching, massaging, and exercising the infant and young child. This physical contact will become mutually enjoyable for both parent and child. Studies of infant development have shown that pleasure in the interaction between the baby and his caretaker is the strongest facilitator of the baby's emotional and physical growth.

Much has been learned from studying the development of infants in different cultures. Whereas an African mother may bounce her infant's feet on her lap starting in the first few days of the baby's life, a Mexican mother may carry her baby bundled up on her back for most of the baby's first year. The African babies show remarkably early mastery of motor skills compared to infants in the Mexican culture or infants in this country. They start to walk as early as six months of age. How a mother in India massages her baby is a special art that has been handed down from generation to generation, communicating love to the infant through the primal language of touch and sensation.

Margaret Mead's studies of different tribes and their child-rearing practices in New Guinea linked the close physical contact between the infants and young children and the adults to the warm and gentle personality characteristics of one tribe. In contrast, another tribe's aggressive, ill-tempered characteristics were linked to the practice of carrying infants in thick baskets, which allowed only minimal physical contact with adults.

All infants have an inborn drive to move. The fetus moves in utero, and a newborn baby who is awake, lying on his back, moves constantly. Some infants are more active; others are quieter and more observant, following objects with their eyes. There are some general developmental lines most of them follow, but each infant has his or her own pace. Development does not follow a straight line; it has ups and downs. An infant who gets excited while learning his first steps might be so absorbed by working on this new task that language development stands still for a while. On the other hand, a baby who babbles all day, working on his first words, might have little energy and interest to master new motor skills. Tamara Meyer emphasizes following the rhythm of the individual child, exercising and massaging according to the child's mood and pace. Her message is that we can create mutually pleasurable activities for parent and child.

This book serves as a general guideline for parents who want to learn ways to encourage their baby's motor development. It builds on the knowledge that exercise during infancy strengthens arm, leg, thigh, and neck muscles, which will help the infant to sit, stand, and walk correctly. But above all it shows parents ways they can communicate love to their child through touch and movement. Time spent together during massage and exercise will become moments of mutual joy and pleasure. Pleasure is the strongest motivating factor in a child's development.

> Irene Chatoor, M.D.
> Pediatrician and Child Psychiatrist
> Director of Consultation and Liaison
> Children's Hospital National Medical Center
> Washington, D.C.

# I
# Benefits of
# Exercise and Massage

# 1
# Why Exercise?

A new and exciting approach has been discovered that will enable parents to enhance their baby's and children's overall development greatly and to build strong and healthy children. It's exercise!

Exercise for adults has now been elevated to near-cult status. No one questions any longer the benefit of jogging, running, jumping, swimming, and stretching to improve our health and well-being. But relatively few parents have yet recognized that exercise, supplemented by massage, is also beneficial for their babies and growing children. It has taken many years for adults to accept exercise in its various forms as advisable and even essential for achieving and maintaining their good health. It may take many more years before they recognize its value for infants and young children.

The reason, in both cases, is ingrained habit and resistance to change. It was not so long ago that runners and joggers, especially women, were regarded as eccentrics when they took to the streets and roads of our cities and towns. Now they are scarcely given a second glance. In time, a similar development may be expected in the case of exercise and massage of babies and youngsters. But parents whose minds open to new research and findings will be among the first to secure the benefits of exercise and massage for their children.

In the past, it was generally assumed that babies would look after themselves as far as exercise was concerned. Nature was left to take its course. Yet now, from the moment the infant appears on the scene, mothers and fathers do everything they can to help nature along. When a baby cries for food, if a mother doesn't supply her own milk, she (or the father) delivers the bottle. When an infant cries for relief from indigestion, his mother or father readily responds.

But when the baby kicks his feet (something he or she starts doing even before birth), parents simply let him go on kicking. There is nothing wrong with that. But there is something more to it. The baby may be signaling a desire to stretch, to exercise, to reach out, and to grow. And I know from personal experience, as do others in the field of child development, that a baby is grateful when someone lends him a hand.

And when nature is left to take its course, is the result necessarily a happy one? What about the ill and cranky babies; those with poor appetites; those who have difficulty in sleeping (giving their parents sleepless nights); those who develop weak backs, poor posture, weak arms and legs? And what about those who lag behind in their intellectual development? And those who become distant and even hostile in their relations with their parents?

The exercise/massage program that I have developed may not take care of all these problems, but it most likely will prove helpful with many of them. As a parent, you will surely be richly rewarded for the time you take in following the relatively simple exercises and massage techniques shown here.

Doctors and therapists in other countries have been ahead of those in the United States in recognizing the value and need of exercise/massage for infants and young children. Some sixty years ago Dr. Detleff Neumann-Neurode of Germany pointed out that in early times the struggle for life had strengthened the human body; but under the impact of modern civilization, with machines replacing human muscles, our bodies have become weaker and more vulnerable. His survey of young children disclosed that 48 percent of the girls and 28 percent of the boys suffered from spine problems.

Since then, with automobiles steadily replacing our legs as a means of locomotion and computers now taking over many of the manual tasks we once performed, the threat to our physical capabilities has become even greater. Dr. Kenneth Cooper, in his book *Aerobics*, has indicated the level to which our youth has sunk, with large numbers turned down for military service because of physical unfitness. Commenting on the examination of military recruits, Cooper writes: "The American myth of the fitness of youth is nowhere more evident than it is on the days when we put new recruits through their first twelve-minute test. Nearly two out of three fail to make it into the good category."[1] (The test determines how far an individual can run in twelve minutes.)

During the 1920s Dr. Neumann-Neurode and a colleague developed a series of exercises designed to counteract the debilitating effects of our industrialized society and our mechanized life. These exercises were based on the belief that certain physical movements would activate the muscles of young children, and would thus provide an answer. They were designed specifically to avert later neuromuscular problems and poor posture—and to correct existing problems. Observing the results in children who had exercised from infancy, the doctors found that they had been successful in sharply reducing the incidence of back problems. At the same time, they found that the intellectual level of the children who had exercised was higher than that of children who had not exercised. They concluded that physical difficulties, resulting from a lack of stimulation and contact with the environment, may also contribute to lower intellectual capacity.

Some years later, Dr. Jaroslav Koch reported the results of his research with infants over a period of twenty-five years at the Institute for the Care of Mother and Child in Prague, Czechoslovakia. He found that those who had exercised had better appetites and had gained weight faster than those who had not; that they slept much better; that they seldom cried, and that, on the whole, they appeared to be more cheerful and much happier. He also found important physical and psychological differences between the two groups. Children stimulated by exercise displayed superior motor development and a greater capacity for learning language. He concluded that physical stimulation develops not only the body but also the mind.

Does it make a difference whether a baby develops earlier or later? Dr. Koch replied with another noteworthy observation:

> Appropriate training will result in a certain rate of an infant's mental development. Lack of stimulation will slow it down. And you cannot expect that a slowly developing child will develop longer and will finally reach the same stage of development as children who develop faster. The development of human beings begins to slow down at a certain age. It even

---

[1]Kenneth Cooper, *Aerobics* (New York: M. Evans and Company, Inc., 1968), 106.

appears that a child who develops slower reaches the limits of his development sooner than a child with a faster rate of development. Since the rate of mental development can be influenced during the infant's first year, this is another reason for intensive care in the upbringing of your child in early infancy.[2]

The idea of exercising babies and young children spread throughout Europe to Australia, Canada, and eventually the United States. A textbook published in the Soviet Union reported that exercise and massage of infants helped to develop a strong immune system and central nervous system. Centers for showing parents how to exercise and massage their babies were soon established in France and other European countries, as well as in Australia. Mothers in Adelaide, Australia, reported that a daily program of exercise and massage had produced a remarkable improvement in the temperament and feeding of their previously irritable and colicky babies. Impressive results were also reported by pediatricians and nurses at the Holy Cross Hospital in Calgary, Canada.

In recent years, a number of American authorities, including Dr. Benjamin Bloom of the University of Chicago and Dr. Burton White, who directed a preschool project at Harvard University, have recognized and endorsed the value of stimulating babies and young children. Dr. White regards the first three years of life, which he describes as "a period of primary importance in the development of a human being," as critical in building a sound foundation for intelligence, creativity, motor coordination, and psychological well-being. During these three years, Dr. White believes, parents can either promote or inhibit their child's growth, depending on how they treat their child. Echoing thoughts of earlier European investigators, Dr. White predicted that "what we now call a normal rate of development will be considered—thirty or forty years from now—to be a slow pace."[3]

Dr. Martin Lorin reported on the results of an investigation of third-grade students in the United States who had had the benefit of physical fitness exercises at an early age: "Those students with more motor proficiency," he wrote, "were found to be less tense, more resourceful, more attentive, and

---

[2]Jaroslav Koch, *Total Baby Development* (New York: Wyden Books, 1976), 15.

[3]Burton White, *The First Three Years of Life* (New York: Prentice-Hall Inc., 1975), 107.

more cooperative. They achieved better in all academic pursuits."[4]

Dr. Lorin and Dr. White both point to the responsibility that parents have for the development of their children during their first few formative years, especially since they hold virtually exclusive control over their children during their preschool years. Dr. Lorin put it this way:

"Only a parent has both the motivation and the opportunity to guide the child's development day in and day out, year after year, from birth to adolescence. During the first five years of life, the critical formative years, 50 to 75 percent of total human contact is likely to be with parents only. Parents should accept responsibility for their child's physical fitness just as they accept responsibility for other aspects of his or her health and well-being."

The most recent research and studies undertaken in the United States reinforce and extend the findings of these earlier investigators. Dr. Mary Ann Fletcher, assistant director of nurseries at George Washington University Hospital in Washington, D.C., reports conclusive evidence that stroking (or massage) has a calming effect on babies, allows them to consume less oxygen, and aids in digestion.

According to Dr. Lynn A. Balzer-Martin, assistant professor of pediatrics at Georgetown University, associated with the Child Development Center in Washington, D.C., "Exercise and massage enhance the development of the three sensory systems that are already quite advanced in newborns and young infants. These three senses are touch (tactile), balance and movement (vestibular), and joint position sense (kinesthesia). These primary sensory systems are particularly important because they mature early and they provide an essential foundation for growth and development in many other areas."

If bonding is not established early, she warned, it could be difficult to achieve it later. The importance of bonding between parents and child has now been widely recognized throughout the world. That the absence of bonding results in future emotional and mental instability has also been well established.

Another authority, Dr. Sidney Cobb, former president of the American Psychosomatic Society and professor emeritus of psychiatry at Brown University, had this to say: "It is now clear that a lot of support in relationships is communicated through physical contact between parent and child."

---

[4]Martin Lorin, *The Parents' Book of Physical Fitness for Children* (New York: Atheneum, 1978), 10.

One of the great benefits that can be claimed for an exercise/massage program is that it will enable parents to establish a happy and health-generating bond with their infants and other children during the most critical formative years. The benefits from such bonding are incalculable and may well run the entire course of the lives of both parents and children.

Many adults have found that exercise helps them in releasing stress and tension. But few seem to realize that the same is true for infants and young children, who are also subject to stress (the topic of a later chapter). There are now scientific data that demonstrate how exercise may relieve stress. In researching the brain's responses to Valium, scientists discovered that the body produces its own Valium-like equivalent. Endorphins are polypeptides that are produced in the brain where they function as neurotransmitters, which are received by specific brain receptors. Their presence in the brain appears to trigger an alert and tranquil response.

Clinical researchers, continuing to explore the effect of endorphins on the body, found that blood samples taken from athletes during and immediately after a workout contained an abundance of these substances. This information has led brain researchers to believe that the feeling of well-being associated with exercise may be due to the overwhelming presence of endorphins in those who are exercising or who have just completed a workout.

The proof of all speculation and research, past and present, is to be found in the experience of professional practice with infants and young children and with their mothers and fathers. My practice over a period of years has resulted in remarkable benefits to all participants in my exercise/massage programs.

One young mother speaks of the increased intimacy she has achieved with her daughter. She finds that since she began exercising with her six-month-old their level of communication has increased dramatically. As she and her daughter move and stretch each day, they look into each other's eyes and achieve a unique sense of communication. She also reports that her daughter is a much happier and more contented baby, crying far less than before. Similar results were reported by other mothers.

Still more striking are the reports received from fathers, who are delighted with the discovery that exercise and massage enable them to establish direct, personal contact with their children. Fathers who hitherto were rather embarrassed, uncomfortable, and squeamish about handling an infant have taken to the exercise/massage program with enthusiasm—and appreciation for a new means of bonding with their babies, with physical and psychological benefit to all concerned.

One man, a very successful lawyer, found himself feeling unusually insecure upon the birth of his first child. "I had spent years in school and nearly seven years building my practice. I thought I could handle anything! However, I felt very squeamish around my new daughter. I knew I loved her from the moment I saw her. But I didn't know how to express it." This man learned of my classes and soon became one of the most frequent participants. "I feel completely at ease now as a father," he says. "I love my daughter and I know that she knows it. Doing exercise with her when I come home and giving a massage now and then has given us a way to communicate and love each other. I can't wait to take her jogging with me!"

One of the things we all discovered at our exercise and massage sessions was that exercise is fun for all the participants, especially for the children. Enjoyment is written on the faces of all the children who appear in the photographs of this book. Their expressions are quite representative, and they serve as the most persuasive endorsement of exercise.

There have also been some unexpected benefits noted by parents participating in classes. One of the mothers bringing her three-month-old daughter to classes was overweight. During the course of the next eight months, the mother became as enthusiastic as her daughter about exercise and managed to lose nearly thirty pounds. The mother has kept her weight off and continues to exercise with her daughter and her husband, who has found their excitement contagious.

The exercises and the massage strokes described in this book may be regarded as part of a preventive health-care program. The idea of preventive health care for adults is gaining increasing acceptance in the United States and abroad, and it is now time to recognize the value of it for children. Exercise and massage are both an invaluable part of preventive health care. By strengthening the muscles and improving the cardiovascular system, they raise our physical level of resistance to disease and stress. The psychological and emotional benefits have already been mentioned.

The earlier you start exercising and massaging your children, the better. You need not be worried about handling your infant, as long as you handle him or her with care and consideration. Babies love—and need—to be touched, and, as mentioned by Dr. White, "there is a great deal of evidence indicating that newborns are beautifully designed to be handled. The parts of the nervous system that are activated by handling are much better developed than those involving the mind, the eyes, and the ears. In addition, handling a baby is clearly one of the few reliable ways of changing a baby's state from distress to apparent comfort."

The program developed in this book is one of the first to take a child from infancy through five years of age—in other words, the entire preschool period during which parents hold virtually complete control. The exercises, divided into four groups, were devised to enhance the natural course of development of your child.

The first group of exercises is for infants up to one year of age. Gentle massage, explained in the subsequent massage section of this book, can be used soon after birth. Certain exercises, as illustrated in the first group, can begin when the baby has developed more strength and has begun to raise his (or her) head.

The newborn baby, having been confined for about nine months in rather cramped quarters, arrives on the scene with limbs drawn up close to the body and in a rather crumpled state. The infant's instinctive impulse is to stretch. The parent comes to his aid by stretching his tiny limbs and encouraging their free movement, thereby easing the infant's transition into the new world.

Exercises during this first period are mostly passive in nature. They are designed to strengthen and relax your baby's arms; to strengthen his abdominal muscles; to strengthen his legs and stimulate his stepping reflex; and to gently exercise his back. Preceding the walking stage, they will help improve your baby's coordination, giving the infant greater strength and confidence in himself when he finally achieves an upright position. And as his muscles and limbs become stronger and more supple, he will feel less frustration in his attempts to move about and finally to walk.

The older infant can be treated to a longer period of stretching and various reflex movements, the joints being gently rotated to encourage neuromuscular development. This helps the baby become familiar with his body and readies him for the next stage of growth. As the baby matures into an active toddler, the exercises change to help develop hand-eye coordination and greater agility. The once helpless infant is fast becoming an adventurer. He learns to crawl, sits unaided, and begins to walk. The exercise program follows his progression, helping to ease transitions by encouraging the self-confidence he needs to accomplish tasks of increasing difficulty.

Parents who have used these exercises have had excellent results. They found that their babies welcomed the gentle stretching of their arms and legs, gurgled contentedly as their knees were raised to the chest, and enjoyed the pressure of mother's or father's hands against the soles of their feet.

After only a few weeks of exercise, parents reported that their babies were eating better, sleeping better, and displaying a more cheerful and happy nature during waking hours—to their great satisfaction. They had every reason to believe that their babies were well on their way to becoming well-adjusted and contented children, building self-confidence and security through the warm feelings of direct physical contact.

The first group of exercises prepares your infant for the next group, designed for ages one to two. About the time of your baby's first birthday, he is ready both physically and psychologically for more active participation in the exercise program. The second series continues to relax and to stretch your baby's limbs while promoting more endurance and strength.

The muscles of the arms are alternately contracted and relaxed; the shoulder joints are rotated, and the muscles of the upper body are brought into play. Gentle pull-ups and stretching help to strengthen your baby's torso. Other exercises stretch and contract the muscles of the legs, work the hip joints, strengthen the ankles, the Achilles tendons, and the feet. This series also introduces exercises to stimulate the cardiovascular system. Other exercises carry forward the program of strengthening your child's back.

These exercises of the first two groups, up to your child's second birthday, are to be handled by either or both parents with care. There should be no abrupt movements at any time in stretching and relaxing the muscles of your infant's arms, legs, neck, and back. Though infants are born with far greater strength than most of us give them credit for, joints and muscles are still relatively weak. This should always be kept in mind, especially since there is a tendency on the part of some parents to become overconfident as the child displays increasing strength, self-assurance, familiarity, and pleasure with the exercises. Furthermore, an abrupt movement is inadvisable at any time and at any age. Be sure to avoid exercises until the prescribed age.

Another important point to be kept in mind, especially during your child's first two years: never force the exercises on your infant or force the pace of your child's development. Exercise must have the acceptance and consent of the child. If your baby is not in the mood, is not interested, or becomes bored, then suspend the exercises. He or she might be more responsive if you switch to a few massage strokes. You can return to the exercise program at a more favorable time.

Always remember that exercise should be pleasurable. Any hint of force or of running against a child's will is almost certain to produce trouble rather than pleasure. Also bear in mind that the purpose of exercise is to promote not only the physical development but the psychological and emotional development as well. These purposes unquestionably are best served in an environment of pleasure and fun. When exercise is enjoyable—as it can and should be—it becomes a welcome lifelong routine and a lifelong source of preventive health care, one that may reduce future medical and hospital bills by thousands and perhaps hundreds of thousands of dollars.

After your child's second birthday, he or she is ready for the more vigorous exercises in the third group, designed for two- to three-year-olds, and in the last group, designed for ages three through five. These series also include aerobic exercise, which stimulates the cardiovascular system.

Among the benefits that can be expected from aerobic exercise, the following were mentioned by Dr. Arthur Weltman, director of the Human Performance Laboratory at the University of Colorado, and Dr. Bryant Stamford, director of the Exercise Physiology Laboratory at the University of Louisville, Kentucky: improved heart circulation and metabolism; more and larger blood vessels; lower heart rate and blood pressure, which reduce the work of the heart at rest and during exercise; a more favorable nerve—hormone balance that may conserve oxygen for the heart muscle; and a reduced level of psychological stress and tension.

The exercises for all four programs are choreographed in such a way that each muscle group is used and then relaxed to provide an evenly balanced workout. This is an important aspect that many exercise programs fail to take into account, leaving children sore and failing to provide overall conditioning.

We have nearly five hundred muscles in our bodies. They usually work in pairs, performing opposite movements. For example, to pull the forearm up to the upper arm, the biceps muscle in front contracts and the triceps muscle in back of the arm relaxes. To straighten the arm, the biceps muscle relaxes while the triceps muscle contracts. It is our ability to use our large muscles and our finer muscles that enables us to perform heavy as well as delicate tasks, such as writing.

Muscles exercised in pairs help to promote proper conditioning. I have provided an overall workout—one that will enhance and promote full and overall development. By strengthening the hundreds of muscles in your child's body and activating his cardiovascular system, these exercise programs should contribute to developing the four major areas of his physical fitness: endurance, strength, agility and coordination, and finally speed.

Just as some parents are too apprehensive about the fragility of an infant, others are very concerned about the ability of older children to sustain forceful exercise. Fitness experts generally agree that both children and adults stand to gain by exerting themselves. It is through the process of exertion that we extend the limits of our strength and build up our bodies.

A Washington, D.C., track coach undertook an investigation to find out why runners on one of his teams were unable to sustain a high rate of speed. After talking with each of them, he came to the conclusion that their failure to be trained to exert themselves as very young children had made it difficult for them to perform at a good level when they reached high school.

Dr. Lorin, in his book, relates the case of a youngster who quit after only three rounds of karate, saying he was tired. An instructor coaxed him into making a greater effort, and he went on to exercise for nearly an hour, pleasantly surprised by the discovery of his hidden resources.

These examples are meant to encourage parents to offer their children a vigorous daily workout, and to gradually and carefully extend the limits of their endurance, using their best judgment to determine what these limits might be. If you have any question regarding your child's participation in the exercise or massage programs, consult your pediatrician.

As mentioned before, the earlier your child begins to exercise, the better. However, you can pick up at any point, selecting the exercise group that fits the age of your child. In the case of families with several children of different ages, different exercise programs will apply.

I have had considerable personal satisfaction in a number of instances where my exercise program became the occasion for enjoyable family social affairs. Mothers and fathers exercise with daughters and sons; brothers and sisters exercise with one another; children exercise with their parents. And all have fun. Exercise has become something they look forward to—a new way for the family not only to get together but, literally, to get closer together.

One mother finds exercise to be invaluable for her two sons, ages five and eight. "Exercise gives them a joyful way of letting go. Often they will both have a lot of pent-up energy. We'll put on music and let them get wild with exercise.

"They love to see their bodies work and move and especially enjoy seeing what their bodies are capable of. At times when they are really tired but their bodies are raring to go, exercises we have learned from the program give them guidelines and help them get centered so that they can relax. Sometimes, exercise takes the edge off a family argument and has us all laughing and feeling happy together again. At other times the kids will grab us both and start working out with us. They really like the exercises. In fact they don't need reminders any longer to remember how they go."

This structured exercise program also affords a unique opportunity for parents who have been separated or divorced to establish a continuing and positive relationship with their child or children. Instead of a strained visitation period, a father and mother might alternate in carrying out the exercises with their child. The father, for example, might take over the exercise program on weekends, during vacation periods, or at other mutually acceptable times. Whatever the arrangement, the important point is that the exercises may continue on a regular basis.

Briefly summing up, this program of exercise, faithfully carried out, should contribute significantly toward helping your child develop strength, health, and well-being, and will offer him a sound basis on which to continue to build a healthy body and mind. Few families—Dr. White puts the figure at "no more than 10 percent"—manage to educate and develop their children satisfactorily during the critical and decisive first years of life. The program presented in this book should help the other 90 percent to join the happy few.

# 2

# Why Massage?

Massage and exercise have some things in common. Yet they are very different. They work on the same areas—the body and the mind. They serve a similar purpose—to improve and to develop physical and mental well-being. Yet they do so in different ways. They complement each other. Together, they give parents a twofold means of developing strong and healthy children.

Some childhood specialists suggest the use of massage for babies and children. Others advocate exercise. For this book I have developed programs of both exercise and massage because I feel there is a need for both, each to be used at different times and to satisfy different needs.

Exercise is an active form of motion to develop the muscles and the cardiovascular system. Though the parent participates and directs the exercise, the child takes an active part in moving his or her arms, legs, and other parts of the body. As the child grows older, he plays an increasingly active role and reaches the point where he is acting on his own, independently of his parent.

In massage, as treated in this book, no such independence is ever reached. Parent and child are always together. Massage is a passive practice. The parent, using his or her hands as an incomparable human instrument, applies them to the infant or the older child, who is in the enviable position of simply lying back and enjoying the treatment.

Exercise is an energetic and assertive activity. Massage soothes, comforts, calms, and refreshes the body. It produces a warm, cozy feeling of relaxation and pleasure—so much so that it often induces sweet sleep.

The two massage programs that follow—one for younger and the other for older children—can be used in different ways. Each can be integrated into the exercise programs, or they can be used entirely independently of the exercise programs. They can be integrated by using some or all of the massage strokes as a preparatory warm-up to exercise and as a wind-down at the conclusion of the exercise program. In the case of strenuous exercise for older children, massage will relax, refresh, and restore tensed and tightened muscles. You can also try alternating the exercise and massage programs. For example, you might exercise with your child for twenty or thirty minutes in the morning, to be followed by twenty or thirty minutes of massage in the evening at bedtime.

From time to time, you may also want to use massage completely independent of, and as a substitute for, exercise. For example, when your baby is cranky and not in the mood for exercise, he or she may be calmed, comforted, and put at ease by the warm strokes of your massaging hands. You will find that massage can often help relieve gastric discomfort. Mothers instinctively apply massage when they burp their babies after feeding them.

And in the case of a transitory emotional or psychological upset, massage again will prove to be a welcome remedy. For example, when your child is highly nervous or disturbed by something beyond your understanding, or if he or she should be aroused from sleep by a bad dream, a parent's comforting and massaging hands can produce wonders. It will take little time for the child to show the benefits he is receiving from both massage and exercise.

One mother told me, "When Hans gets keyed up, you just can't talk him out of it. At these times, touching him, rubbing his back, helps him to let go and relax. At bedtime Hans often has difficulty going to sleep. He is often overexcited or overtired. Massage relieves him. When Carl or I massage Hans, there is no need for words and our hands help him relax so that he can sleep."

She mentioned that massage was particularly helpful in easing a case of pneumonia: "Hans felt terrible. We began massaging him as soon as the illness set in, and this made him feel more comfortable. His doctor was impressed with Hans's quick recovery."

Hans, who is seven, tells me he likes massage. "Sometimes massage makes me feel kind of tired at bedtime and helps me fall asleep. When I'm sick, and I feel unhappy because I have to stay in bed, Mommy or Daddy gives me a massage and it makes me feel fine again."

Massage is said to be as old as mankind itself. And this may have something to do with the fact that massage is intimately related to birth. It provides a means of continuing bodily contact between mother and child following the birth of a baby. The need for physical contact has been well established by scientists and researchers in the United States and foreign countries.

As expressed by Ashley Montagu, the well-known anthropologist:

> The process of birth represents a prolonged series of shocks which every infant experiences, and nothing exists more powerfully calculated to assuage the effect of those shocks than the fondling and nursing the mother is designed to give the child as immediately after birth as possible. When afforded such reassurance through the skin, the effects of the shock of birth are gradually mitigated. But if the infant is not afforded such an alleviation of his shock, the effects of that shock will continue and will more or less affect his subsequent growth and development.[1]

He quotes J. Lionel Taylor, in *The Stages of Human Life*: "The greatest sense in our body is our touch sense. . . . We feel, we love and hate, are touchy and are touched, through the touch corpuscles of our skin."

Humans and other animals certainly feel before they begin to think. They communicate through the sense of touch before and after birth, and later it is through touching that we humans communicate our feelings. By cradling, cuddling, and rocking a baby, the parent assures the child of security, warmth, and love. Massage serves a similar function through stimulation of the skin, bringing both physical and psychological benefits.

Experiments with monkeys and other animals indicate that infants who had been neglected by their mothers were ill-tempered, maladjusted, and even physically inferior to those who had been coddled. The findings also hold for human beings.

---

[1]Ashley Montagu, *Touching: The Human Significance of the Skin*, 2d ed. (New York: Harper & Row, 1978), 192.

*17*

According to Montagu, "Adequate tactile satisfaction during infancy and childhood is of fundamental importance for the subsequent healthy behavioral development of the individual. The experimental and other research findings on other animals, as well as those on humans, show that tactile deprivation in infancy usually results in behavioral inadequacies in later life. . . . It should be evident that in the development of the person tactile stimulation should begin with the newborn baby."

Montagu cites the work of other researchers to support the conclusion that children who have been "maternally deprived" have been disturbed in both their physical and mental growth. He relates the case of a deprived three-year-old child whose bone growth was only half that of a normal child. That being the case, massage offers mothers and fathers the means of securing sound physical contact with their children.

The beneficial effects of massage have been recorded in early history. Dr. Douglas Graham, in his *Treatise on Massage*, pointed out that "massage has been partly practiced from the most ancient times, among savage and civilized nations, in some form of rubbing, anointing, kneading, percussing, passive or mixed movements."[2]

Going back to about 1000 B.C., we find in Homer's *Odyssey* a reference to beautiful women who rubbed and anointed war-weary heroes to rest and refresh them. Among ancient Greeks and Romans, according to Dr. Graham, massage was widely practiced by people of different classes, from the patricians and the wealthy down to the poor and the slaves. For some, massage was a means of hastening convalescence; for others, it was used to restore muscles in preparation for undertaking severe tests of strength.

Athletes and gladiators were massaged both to relieve the pains of bruises and to reinvigorate their muscles. In the fifth century B.C. Herodicus, one of the masters of Hippocrates, the father of medicine, required that his patients exercise and have their bodies rubbed. Herodotus, called the father of history, recorded instructions for massage in ancient Egypt: at first, the friction should be gentle and slow; then it should become rapid and accompanied by pressure; toward the end, the friction should again become gentle.

"Frictions" were said to have been so widely used at one time in Egypt that "no one retires from the bath without being rubbed."

---

[2]Douglas Graham, *A Practical Treatise on Massage* (New York: William Wood & Co., 1884), 3.

Practically all countries and all parts of the world, including India, China, Japan, Russia, western Europe, Africa, and Latin America, have reported the practice and beneficial results of massage. Early practitioners did not know why or how it was that "frictions" and "rubbings" produced these results, but they were sufficiently satisfied with them to continue the practice through the ages.

Scientists have been trying for years to learn exactly why massage holds the magical property of dissipating fatigue and restoring tired muscles. As far back as 1881, Dr. Zabludowski, professor of massage at the University of Berlin, conducted a series of experiments with frogs, which are notable for the large muscles in their legs. He exhausted their legs by a series of rhythmic contractions. The group that was massaged afterward soon regained their lost vigor. The other, which was not, remained exhausted.

Dr. Zabludowski then tested the muscles of human beings. He had one man lift a 2.2-pound weight as many times as he could. He lifted the weight 840 times at one-second intervals and then became exhausted. After his arm had been massaged five minutes, he proceeded to lift the same weight 1,100 times.[3]

The interpretation given to results of this kind was that massage stimulation increased muscle endurance and removed lactic acid from exhausted muscles.

The beneficial effect of massage on the circulatory system is attributed to the fact that it stimulates capillaries and circulation, and generally increases the speed of circulation. Since blood flows more rapidly through an area that is massaged (one experiment showed that it flowed three times more rapidly) there is an increase in the interchange between the blood and the tissues.

As for the effects of massage on the psyche, these are more easily seen than their causes are understood. Recently, a brain research scientist from NIH (National Institutes of Health) attended one of my massage workshops. During the course of a series of relaxation holds (which are taught in the chapters on massage) she suddenly opened her eyes. "This is truly an endorphinergic experience," she said as she closed her eyes again to savor the feeling.

Whether or not endorphins, the substances produced by the brain that cause one to feel a sense of well-being, are involved in the process of massage is

---

[3]Ibid., 74.

not yet documented. However, most adults and children will agree with this scientist that massage greatly relaxes the mind as well as the body.

While all these extraordinary results may be recognized, it remains for other medical researchers of the future to discover what produces them. Meanwhile, the idea of massaging babies and young children is growing in popularity in all parts of the world. Centers have been established in Germany, Sweden, and Australia to show mothers and fathers how to massage their young. Parents are learning that in countries such as India massage of babies has been a tradition for centuries. They are being informed of mothers in Bali who massage their babies from the second day of birth—which may result in the beauty of the Balinese, which has been recognized throughout the world.

The movement toward massage has now taken hold in the United States, where I and other specialists are providing instruction to parents. I have made a special effort to bring fathers to my workshops, impressing on them the value of massage as a means of bonding and establishing physical contact with their offspring. Mothers instinctively embrace their babies. Not so with fathers, who often feel embarrassed, uncomfortable, and self-conscious about taking physical possession of their newborn. Massage as well as exercise offers a natural and purposeful way of doing so.

The early Puritan tradition regarding the body as something to be treated with extreme reserve—as if it were sinful, untouchable, potentially harmful—discouraged physical contact among Americans and is believed to be responsible in good measure for the aloofness, the inhibitions, and the mental disorders of not a few Americans today. The practice of putting our babies in playpens has contributed to this mental attitude of separation. While the pen is useful in keeping a baby out of one kind of trouble—physical harm—it may plunge him into another kind—a feeling of isolation, of loneliness, of being abandoned to a new, mysterious, and seemingly unfriendly world.

The trend among informed and enlightened parents is to liberate their babies from the playpen; to pick them up, cuddle, and caress them when they are crying in order to reassure them that they have nothing to fear; that there is always someone ready to answer their needs, and that all is right with the world. Many parents have discovered an alternative to and a great improvement over the playpen. It is the baby carrier made of soft material, which allows the baby to sit snugly on the back or stomach of his mother or father as one or the other goes about her or his business.

A psychologist friend is a strong advocate of massage as a way of communicating loving care to children and of bringing human beings closer together through the magic of touch. And it can prove to be useful in special cases, such as the following:

A newly remarried man I know found himself in an extremely uncomfortable and unhappy situation when he was being rejected by his four-year-old stepdaughter, naturally grieving over the loss of her father. I encouraged him to seek out an opportunity to try massage as a means of breaking down her resentment and coming closer to her. One night, noticing that his stepdaughter was having difficulty falling asleep, he offered to rub her back. She agreed, soon relaxed, and fell into a pleasurable sleep. Since then, she has been looking forward to her stepfather's massage before falling to sleep each night; and they have become warm friends.

Another special case is that of premature babies. Recent studies in the United States, Canada, and Sweden disclosed that these infants responded most favorably to daily massage and exercise, administered by a nurse or volunteer aide. Premature babies usually do not receive the cuddling and handling enjoyed by full-term babies. They are whisked away and held in isolation in high-technology nurseries. The cuddling and massage provided by the surrogate mothers in the recent experiments produced these results: the premature babies gained more weight, ate and eliminated more easily, and proved to be more robust than the prematures babies who did not have the benefit of this innovative care.

The results of this research substantiated what other researchers and doctors had previously reported: tactile stimulation helps babies and older children to assimilate food, to gain weight more readily, which in turn helps to strengthen their immune systems so that they can be in a stronger position to ward off disease.

Massage has also been found helpful in soothing babies who are teething and suffering from colds. It has been effective in relieving symptoms of colic. Sue Fortunato found that massage greatly relieved her colicky son. "Pyare cried with great intensity from the time he was born. I was at first at a loss in finding anything to relieve him. Bathing helped a little. I felt very frustrated and upset that my first beautiful baby was so ill at ease.

"After a few weeks I learned about massage and felt intuitively that this might work with him. I began massaging him each day at bathtime and whenever he was upset. His colic continued for a long time, but he became much more relaxed than before. His crying, which was very intense at times, seemed to make him stiff. After I began using massage, I noticed this change as he became more cuddly and relaxed.

"During this time I also felt something wonderful happening to me. I finally began to enjoy being a mother. Massage seemed to bring us close together. I felt a real connection with him that increased daily. I think that massage is something unique for babies. We all cuddle them and play with them, but massage is something more. It seems to give the baby good positive messages about his body. It helped me feel completely comfortable with him and helped him feel completely comfortable with himself."

There is another valuable feature to massage: it's fun! Children love it, and parents enjoy the satisfaction their children derive from their handwork. This health-giving interchange creates a climate of pleasure and well-being that the child, from infancy, associates with his parents—the source of his gratification.

The lifelong psychological and behavioral benefits that flow from such an association are easy to imagine. Dr. Hallie Lovitt, a psychologist and mother, with her husband, also a psychotherapist, began using massage with their children from the time they were born.

Now eight and eleven, her two sons still ask for back rubs and happily give them as well. Dr. Lovitt sees her sons as having benefitted from massage. Although many eleven-year-olds feel uncomfortable with their bodies, her son is at ease with himself. Both children are warm and affectionate. Massage, she feels, has made touching easy and natural in her family.

According to Dr. Lovitt, massage helps children with identity issues. Lovingly massaged children come to feel good about their bodies. Conversely, she finds that adult patients who were abused children often have difficulty accepting and feeling good about themselves. Most importantly, Dr. Lovitt feels that massage instruction gives these adults in particular, as well as others, an opportunity to bond with their children.

This aspect should make baby massage all the more valuable in a society where both parents often find it necessary to take full-time jobs, leaving them less time with their children at home. Massage is a means of securing maximum value per limited minute with your baby and other children.

I first became interested in massaging children some years ago. I was working with four hyperactive two-year-olds enrolled in a preschool program.

As a massage therapist, I had been successful in helping adults suffering from chronic stress. I thought I might enable the children to relax by applying some of the techniques I was using for adults.

I had the impression that these children had never really relaxed, and I decided I would first try to get them to rest during a two-hour nap period. I began by joining them in running around the track, a daily routine. Then, when they were in their cots for their naps, I went to each one, gently massaged their shoulders, and applied the "relaxation hold" (which you will find at the opening of the massage program described in subsequent chapters).

The first day the children all laughed. They thought it was funny. The next day they were competing with one another to be first to receive the massage. On the third day, three of the children fell asleep after treatment, including a boy who had never been able to nap before. On subsequent days, the children settled down and became calm—a notable improvement over their previous condition.

Having been successful with these hyperactive children, I went on to apply these techniques to other children. I soon began to receive enthusiastic reports from their parents. The children cried less; they were eating better and gaining weight; they slept better, looked better, and seemed to be more content. Mothers and fathers felt more fulfilled as parents. That's when I regularly began teaching parents the art of baby and child massage. The techniques are described in Part III. They can be followed easily by mothers and fathers who take the time and trouble to help their children—and help themselves in the process.

# 3

# Bonding by Exercise and Massage

The bond between parents and their baby is a unique force that often endures a lifetime. It has the extraordinary effect of blessing those who are touched by it. Its absence or denial has had the terrible effect of crippling human beings both physically and mentally—even to the point of causing death.

Until quite recently, little attention was paid to the bonding process during the critical periods immediately after birth and during childhood. Pediatricians focused on correct feeding and separation of newborn infants from their mothers. Hospitals and nurses feared the spread of germs and so confined infants to virtual isolation wards. Another theory was that fondling and caressing children would "spoil" them.

Today researchers in the field of child development have come to the conclusion that handling a baby fulfills a biological and psychological need of both the infant and the parent. Through the interplay of touching and cradling, the mother and father are able to express to their baby their feelings of love and dedication. The baby is held and comforted when he or she cries. His hunger is satisfied at the breast or bottle as he is held close, and he is kept warm near his mother's body. This physical contact is a primary ingredient in creating the attachment between parent and child.

That tactile stimulation or touching should play such a vital role in promoting this first bond should not be surprising. Touch is the first sense to develop in the unborn child. And it is through the tactile sense that the infant first experiences the world outside the womb. In being touched, the infant is made to feel secure and loved.

This first experience of being loved and nurtured creates a strong impression that influences social interactions in later life. As adults, we express ourselves and feel loved through the sense of touch. We even describe ourselves in tactile terms—we are touchy or cold in our reactions to one another.

Growing awareness of the importance of bonding and of physical contact between parent and child from the very moment of birth produced a revolution in maternity care in the United States. Drs. Marshall H. Klaus and John H. Kennell, who are credited with being among the pioneers in reopening the previously sealed hospital nurseries, maintain that "this revolt against professional medical practices is unprecedented." As a result, more and more parents are taking physical possession of their infants at birth; fathers attend the birth of their babies; infants are allowed to remain with their mothers at the hospital; many are having their babies at home, weighing the benefits of intimacy and freedom from the outside control of nurses, doctors, and hospitals against the risks of an emergency that might require hospital care; and many are now breast-feeding their babies—possibly one of the most powerful factors in the bond between mother and child.

Scientists continue to explore the nature of the bonding phenomenon. In one study, infants and mothers were observed at the time of birth and at intervals to the age of three months. Half of the mothers were allowed to spend as much time as they liked with their babies immediately after birth. The other half were separated from their babies for several hours after birth. The results recorded at the end of the three-month period were striking: infants and mothers in the first group—the ones who had remained together after birth—displayed far greater responsiveness and affection to each other than did those in the other group.

Klaus and Kennell, in their important work on the subject, *Parent-Infant Bonding*, described a number of interactions that produce satisfaction for the mother as well as her infant immediately after birth. For example, when the infant takes his mother's breast, "his sucking, in turn, is pleasurable to both of them."[1] Among the first interactions between mother and child are touch

---

[1]Marshall H. Klaus and John H. Kennell, *Parent-Infant Bonding* (St. Louis: The C. V. Mosby Company, 1982), 56.

and eye-to-eye contact. They cited the following experiment to demonstrate the tactile relationship:

Thirteen nude infants were placed next to their mothers a few minutes or hours after birth. Most mothers proceeded to touch them, first with their fingertips and then with their palms, massaging and stroking the newborn babies. Another study of infants born at home reported a similar pattern: mothers instinctively begin touching and then massaging their babies immediately after birth. The conclusion drawn from these studies is that touching and cuddling, especially at the beginning of the infant's life, play an important role in bonding the mother to her child and in giving her infant a welcome into his new world.

Klaus and Kennell offer this recommendation on touching immediately after birth:

> We believe that there is strong evidence that at least 30 to 60 minutes of early contact in privacy should be provided for every parent and infant to enhance the bonding experience. Studies have not clarified how much of the effect may be apportioned to the first hours and how much to the first days, but it would appear that additional contact in both periods will probably help mothers become attached to their babies. For some mothers, one period may be more important than the other. If the health of the mother or infant makes this impossible, then discussion, support, and reassurance should help the parents appreciate that they can become as completely attached to their infant as if they had the usual bonding experience, although it may require more time and effort. . . . We also strongly urge that the infant remain with the mother as long as she wishes throughout the hospital stay so that she and the baby can get to know each other. We believe that in the near future, placement in the large central nursery will be phased out for most babies. Allowing the infant to be with the mother will permit both mother and father to experience longer periods to learn about their baby and to develop a strong tie in the first week of life.

What about premature babies who have to be placed in an incubator and cannot be left with their mothers to be cuddled and massaged? Psychologist Ruth Rice sought to overcome this handicap with an experiment in Dallas. She had nurses instruct fifteen mothers in stroking and massaging infants upon their release from the hospital. The mothers treated their children four times a day, fifteen minutes each time, for a month. The infants, examined when they were four months old, were found to have advanced further neurologically and physically than premature infants who had not been treated. They gained more weight and scored higher in mental functioning. Rice recommended that mothers be allowed to cuddle and massage their premature babies while they were still in the incubator—an approach now recommended by most doctors and staff.[2]

Nurse Patricia Rausch recently reported the results of an experiment with forty premature infants divided into two equal groups. One group was massaged fifteen minutes a day for ten days. The other received only routine hospital care for premature children. The results showed that the infants who had been massaged gained more weight than those in the other group. The experiment also indicated that massage had promoted the elimination of waste matter, thereby decreasing gastric and abdominal discomforts.[3]

Recognizing the value of massage, the Holy Cross Hospital in Calgary, Canada, developed a volunteer "Cuddlers Program" to provide physical stimulation to infants who otherwise would have been denied its benefits. Twenty volunteers, ranging in age from twenty to seventy-five years, were enlisted to serve as substitutes for mothers who were unable to attend premature or otherwise hospitalized infants, babies who were awaiting adoption, and others who could not be served by fully occupied nurses. After being shown how to massage, exercise, and otherwise stimulate the infants, the volunteers were each entrusted with the care of a child. As in the case of bonding, the program proved satisfying to the surrogate as well as to the infant, and the hospital had a waiting list of volunteers desiring to cuddle and massage babies.[4]

Experiments with sheep, goats, and monkeys support the view that tactile stimulation and bonding between mother and offspring operate throughout the animal kingdom. As expressed by Montagu, "It is evident that in mammals generally cutaneous stimulation is important to all stages of development, but particularly important during the early days of the life of the newborn, during pregnancy, during labor, delivery, and during the nursing period."

---

[2]Ruth Rice, "Child Development." *Psychology Today* (January 1981).

[3]Patricia Bodolf Rausch, MSN, "Effects of Tactile and Kinesthetic Stimulation on Premature Infants." *JOGN Nursing* (January-February 1981): 34–36.

[4]Joanne DeForest and Anne Porter, "Cuddlers: A Volunteer Infant Stimulation Program." *The Canadian Nurse* (July-August 1981), 38–40.

Bonding, of course, originates with the mother, since she is the one who bears the infant and nurtures him upon entry into the outside world. The bond between mother and child is unquestionably unique. The physical tie, by nature, may be said to give the mother primacy, leaving the father somewhat on the sidelines, as expectant spectator. But primacy does not mean exclusivity; the father, too, feels a strong bond with his offspring. Until recently, this was largely ignored in the United States. In the process of reproduction, the male was regarded as having served his function when his mate became pregnant. After that, she and the infant were the concern of doctors, nurses, and the hospital establishment. The father was left aside, as someone who need not be directly involved in what was going on.

All that is now changing and is part of what Klaus and Kennell described as the revolution in maternity care. The American father, following the precedent of his opposite numbers in Europe and other parts of the world, is asserting himself in the hospital and is turning up in increasing numbers in the delivery room. He is there not only to support the mother but also to be on the scene to hold his baby as soon as he or she appears. Prince Charles demonstrated to the world that even royalty may opt for fatherly attendance at births when he attended the birth of his son, Prince William.

The dramatic change in the status of the American father came home to me one day when a client related his experience of becoming a father. When he awaited the birth of his first child some twenty years ago, he said, he was very excited at the prospect of becoming a father and raising a family, but when his daughter was born, he found himself outside the birth process, as if he were little more than just another onlooker.

When finally he was allowed to hold his daughter, he felt uneasy and uncomfortable, and fearful that he might do something to harm her. She seemed so tiny and vulnerable. Also, he was given to understand that fathers were not expected to have much contact with their babies. In the years that followed, he related, he tried to be a good father to his daughter and two subsequent children, providing for them as best he could, but something was missing—he felt he hardly knew his children. Now, recently remarried and again a father, things were very different. Having learned about the importance of establishing and cultivating a bond with a child as soon after birth as possible, he was present while his baby was being born, helping his wife through some of the most difficult moments of labor. Since his wife was too exhausted to receive the infant, his arms were the first to hold the baby. He described this as one of the most exciting moments of his life. He no longer felt uneasy about holding a baby. The original bond established at birth has been strengthened by daily contact with his new daughter. As an involved father, he does not miss an opportunity to cuddle and to play with his new child and is convinced that close physical contact from birth has contributed greatly to the loving relations he enjoys with her.

Dr. Lee Salk observed that fathers are now looking for greater involvement with their children. "Men have always had a need to be tender and to nurture," he remarked. "Now society is allowing it to emerge." Psychologist Avodah Offit agrees, saying, "Fatherhood is the new family romance of the eighties." Men seem to be taking to this modern approach to fatherhood with the same gusto that women are moving into the working world outside the home. Steve Bogira, a father and writer who began a "nurturant fathers" group in Chicago, feels that "just as women need assertiveness training in the workplace, men need assertiveness training at home."[5]

A psychologist friend told me that one of his strongest and fondest memories of his childhood was the time he would ride in the car with his father. As they chatted, his father would pat him on the knee or on the back. These pats let him know that his father loved him and cared deeply for him. "Don't ask me why," he said, "but these pats on the knee meant more to me than almost anything else my father did for me."

My friend's father grew up during an age when touching was taboo, and children—especially boys—were not supposed to receive too much affection. This taboo—so remote from the practice in many parts of Europe and Latin America, where fathers embrace their sons as well as their daughters at all ages—had its public champion in the person of Dr. Luther Emmett Holt, considered to be the outstanding child-rearing expert at the turn of this century. Holt warned mothers against ruining their babies and children by such practices as cuddling and rocking them in rocking chairs or cradles, or picking them up when they cried. He suggested that such practices, including breast-feeding (not considered sanitary or civilized for well-bred women), were rather primitive and likely to lead to a generation of weak, uncivilized men and women. These ideas led to a war against the cradle and the rocking chair, and the

---

[5]L. Langway et al., "A New Kind of Father." *Newsweek* 98 (November 30, 1981): 93 ff.

eventual replacement of the cradle by the stationary, nonrocking crib, to which the baby was condemned in isolation until given his bottle at fixed, regimented hours. If he cried, there was to be no response, and the afflicted mother, to do her duty, was to let him go on crying. As a result, Ashley Montagu says, "millions of mothers sat and cried along with their babies."

In time, a reaction set in against this mechanistic and even inhumane treatment of children, particularly when it was observed that the denial of physical contact in the form of parental handling and cuddling appeared to be related to a widespread disease called "marasmus" or infantile debility. Several pediatricians introduced the practice of "mothering" in their hospitals. One of them established the rule that every baby should be picked up and "mothered" several times a day. Montagu reported that, following the institution of "mothering" at Bellevue Hospital in New York City, the mortality rate for infants less than one year of age fell from about 30 percent to less than 10 percent. According to Montagu:

> What the child requires if it is to prosper, it was found, is to be handled, and carried, and caressed, and cuddled, and cooed to, even if it isn't breast-fed. It is the handling, the carrying, the caressing, and the cuddling that we would here emphasize, for it would seem that even in the absence of a great deal else, these are the reassuringly basic experiences the infant must enjoy if it is to survive in some semblance of health. Extreme sensory deprivation in other respects, such as light and sound, can be survived, as long as the sensory experiences at the skin are maintained.

Dr. Brock Chisholm, former director of the World Health Organization, was greatly impressed by the "cradle" practices he found in a maternity ward he visited in Pakistan, and he was disturbed when he found that authorities were thinking of dropping their "old-fashioned" methods and importing the "modernized," "sanitized," and isolated American crib. Reporting on his Pakistan visit, Dr. Chisholm wrote:

> I saw the best maternity ward I have ever seen in any country, far better than I have ever seen in North America. Here was a big maternity ward with beds down both sides. The foot posts of each bed were extended up about three feet or so, and slung between the foot posts was a cradle. The baby was in the cradle, and I noticed as I looked down the ward that one squeak out of the baby and up would come the mother's foot, and with her

toe she would rock the cradle. On the second squeak, which showed that the baby was really awake, she would reach into the cradle and take the baby into her arms, where a baby is supposed to be most of the time.[6]

The Pakistani authorities may have had second thoughts when they learned of Dr. Chisholm's criticism of their intentions: "They wanted to get rid of that perfectly beautiful arrangement, to put their babies under glass the way we do, and to keep them in inspection wards where they can be seen at a distance by their loving fathers whenever they visit, and taken to their mother if she is good and does as the nurse tells her. They wanted to do all that because we Westerners had given them the impression that all our methods are superior to theirs."

Discussing the subject, Montagu raises some very serious considerations:

One cannot help wondering whether the unexplained occurrence of "crib death," or "the sudden infant death syndrome," that is, the finding dead in its cot of a baby who has been perfectly healthy and for whose death no cause can be found, may not, at least in part, be due to inadequate sensory stimulation, particularly tactile stimulation. Inadequate sensory stimulation may not be the only factor involved in crib deaths, but it may well be a predisposing factor. It is rare for a child over one year to be found dead unexpectedly. Most crib deaths occur in infants between one and six months. It would be interesting to know what the incidence of sudden infant death would be in cradle-raised as compared with cot-raised babies.[7]

Less serious but nonetheless disturbing symptoms have been attributed to neglect in the form of inadequate body contact with the infant. Eczema, among other disorders, has been attributed in some cases to physical/emotional disturbance in an infant who suffers from lack of physical contact with his parents. Dr. Maurice Rosenthal examined twenty-five children with eczema. He found that a majority had not been cuddled or handled very much by their parents. In Australia, infant eczema has been reported to have been treated successfully by regular tactile stimulation.

---

[6]Ashley Montagu, *Touching: The Human Significance of the Skin*, 2d ed. (New York: Harper & Row, 1978), 84.

[7]Ibid., 129.

The programs of massage and exercise described in Parts II and III of this book will be useful to mothers and fathers in dealing with many of the points raised in this chapter. Massage, especially, provides an excellent way to continue and to deepen the bond parents may have established with their child at birth. And in those cases where parents have failed to establish an early bond, medical experts offer assurances that it is never too late to correct the situation; there is no need to carry a guilt-ridden conscience. Perhaps there is no better way of "catching up" on bonding than by massaging and exercising your child. You can start at any time, and at any age; the sooner, the better.

The need to catch up applies to those mothers who have been handicapped by the outmoded practices of such discredited anticradle and anticuddling crusaders as Dr. Holt. It applies to both mothers and fathers who, in cases of cesarean section, had to be separated in the hospital from their infant. And it applies, perhaps very urgently, to those parents who have adopted a child with whom they want to establish a close and loving bond as soon as possible. The same is true, as indicated by a personal experience I related earlier, for newly reorganized families arising from divorce and remarriage of one or both parents, one or both bringing children from a previous marriage into the new family.

I have received encouraging words of gratitude from parents in these many different circumstances who have come to my offices for help in bonding and deepening their relations with their biological or adopted children through my programs of massage and exercise.

# 4

# Relieving Children's Stress

Never before has stress received so much attention. Medical journals, magazines, books, TV programs, and clinics across the country describe stress as the number-one threat to our well-being. We find that it figures prominently in America's high rate of immune-system diseases and psychosomatic illnesses. Divorce rates, approaching the 50 percent mark, are blamed, in part, on stress. Automobile accidents, suicides, and crime can often be traced to stress in the lives of victims and their assailants.

Anxiety, depression, and chronic fatigue, all symptoms of stress, have been treated by psychologists and psychiatrists with therapy and drugs. They are now also using new creative therapies, notably exercise, massage, and nutrition.

Some years ago I worked with a group of physicians who specialized in holistic medicine, providing a relaxation treatment and training program for patients suffering from stress. When the patients came to see me, many had serious mental and physical health problems due, in part, to the toll that stress was taking. After discussing stress and coming to understand the effect that stressors were having on their lives, most patients became enthusiastic about embarking on the program. First they came for weekly or biweekly treatments that involved massage and relaxation holds similar to those presented in this book. I then taught them relaxation postures that they could do at home, in the office, or in transit. Finally, we worked together to design a suitable daily exercise program. Over time, many patients improved dramatically. Some were able to discontinue medication and many claimed improved efficiency at work and a healthier family life. Many of these people could have been spared years of ill health, difficult marriages, and psychological problems if they had known the key to relaxation and had had the tools to deal with stress at an early age. I then began thinking of using this program with children.

Though it is a burgeoning problem for millions of Americans, we largely ignore the signs of stress where they first begin to appear—in our infants and children. We are inclined to think of childhood as an idyllic period. Child experts are exploding this myth. Children are under stress. In fact, Mary Miller, in one of the first books published on the subject, *Child Stress*, demonstrates that children experience stress in the same degree as their parents. (See chart on pages 39–40.)

It is time to take a serious look at childhood stress. Its effects are cumulative. Since the first years of a person's life are the formative years, the earlier a child learns to cope with stress, aided by sensitive and understanding parents, the less likely are his or her chances of becoming a victim of stress as an adult. The lessons learned in childhood can be applied through adolescence and into adulthood. Parents can learn to detect the stress signals of their children and they can apply effective methods for helping their children to cope with stress through exercise and massage. But let us first take a look at stress to better understand what it is and how it affects us.

Stress is not limited to the latter part of the twentieth century. Our primitive ancestors relied on their ability either to flee from or to attack those who threatened their lives. Their bodies prepared them for the dangerous test before them. Although we are seldom threatened by wild animals or assailants bearing weapons, we are nevertheless affected by stress on a daily basis.

According to Dr. Hans Selye, well-known expert on stress and its effects, "Stress is the nonspecific response of the body to any demand made upon it."[1] Dr. Selye believes there are three stages of stress. The first, or Alarm stage, occurs as a result of threat or perceived threat. When the brain registers a stressful situation, a message is sent to the pituitary glands. There, a hormone

---

[1]Hans Selye, *The Stress of Life* (New York: McGraw-Hill, 1976).

called adrenocorticotrophic hormone (ACTH) is manufactured. This hormone travels through the circulatory system where it activates the adrenal glands to produce adrenaline and other hormones. These hormones quickly act, causing the body's many systems to prepare for fast, forceful action. They cause the kidneys and the digestive system to slow down or stop functioning, allowing the body's resources to go, instead, to those organs needed for the threatening encounter. Sugars and fats are released into the bloodstream to provide additional energy. Heart and lung rates increase dramatically to prepare the body for strenuous activity. Additionally, blood-clotting mechanisms increase their effectiveness to be ready for any injury that may occur as a result of the threat. One's hearing and long-range sight become more acute to assist in the fight or flight that may ensue. These miraculous adaptations, handed down through the millennia, have allowed the human race to survive and prosper.

Next is the Resistance stage. This is the leveling-off period that occurs after the threat has disappeared. Now the body's systems return to normal. Heart and lung activity decrease and normalize. Muscles, which were flexed, readying the subject for action, relax. The digestive system that had stopped functioning resumes its normal capacity, as do the kidneys. Long-range vision and blood-clotting mechanisms return to normal.

When the body is not allowed to return to its normal condition or is taxed by stress over a long period of time, the Exhaustion stage sets in. This stage can have serious repercussions. Stomach ulcers, blood clots, hypertension, and high blood pressure may occur as a result of this prolonged wear and tear on the body. Chronic emotional problems may also appear.

Since stress can bring on illness and even death, the challenge of living in this century is to learn how to cope with stress effectively. We can best begin by realizing that stress is evident in the lives of infants and young children. Any parent who has tried to comfort a screaming newborn knows this intuitively. Quite simply, babies communicate their distress by crying. What makes a baby cry? Why is a baby distressed? Do different cries mean different things?

Most parents have their own ideas of what makes their baby cry. It is usually assumed that the baby is hungry or tired. The fact is that babies have an urgent need for close physical contact, the lack of which causes distress and leads to their crying. Often a baby's crying will bring the close physical contact of the mother. In his theory on bonding and attachment, John Bowlby stresses the importance of the crying behavior and subsequent mothering as part of an intricate system that evolved for the sole purpose of protecting the baby from harm. In Dr. Harry Harlow's famous experiment, baby monkeys surprised researchers by showing their preference for a cloth-covered wire facsimile "mother monkey" over a plain wire "monkey," even though the plain wire monkey "lactated." These monkeys demonstrated that "contact comfort," as Harlow termed it, is more important to the baby than food, in this instance at least.[2]

Margaret Mead, in her comparative study of two neighboring tribes of New Guinea, supported the premise that babies deprived of close physical contact will later demonstrate aggression, a common symptom of stress. The Arapesh, a mountain-dwelling tribe, treat their young to almost constant physical contact. The baby is nursed before he becomes hungry. He is held in close contact at all times and is kept from crying at all cost. Arapesh children feel comfortable with and trust most of the adult tribe members. This is due to the fact that both men and women exhibit maternal instincts by being demonstrative with the infants. Margaret Mead describes the Arapesh people as being warm and gentle.

In the river valley below live the Mungdamoor. Their babies are fed after showing considerable distress, with little affection. They are carried in thick baskets that allow for little physical contact with the mother. Margaret Mead described the Mungdamoor as an aggressive, ill-tempered people.[3]

We do not need to look as far as New Guinea to see evidence of a baby's need for contact-comfort. Some babies will cry to show distress when being undressed. They seem to need the feeling of being wrapped in clothes. They are comforted when wrapped in a towel or blanket, just tightly enough to give a feeling of firm contact.

At times when a baby can be comforted in no other way, a gentle massage may prove successful in easing distress. The discomfort caused by teething can also be soothed away with massage. Exercise, largely passive at this early stage, is often the perfect antidote to moodiness. Babies seem more relaxed and at ease after exercise. Used together, massage and exercise work remarkably well to combat baby stress.

In the next stage—that of youth—stress continues to be a serious factor

---

[2]Judy Dunn, *Distress and Comfort* (Cambridge: Harvard University Press, 1977).

[3]Ibid.

in daily life. The pain of children, their anger and their fears, are all very real. Many events that cause children to experience stress are similar to those that affect adults. Drs. Thomas Holms and Richard Rahe devised a stress chart for adults. Forty-three life situations and events are listed with a corresponding numerical score of the stress potential for each. You need only look at the chart and add up the score to determine whether yours is a moderate, medium, or severe level of stress. Mary Miller, in *Child Stress*, lists forty-three similar life events and their corresponding numerical stress scores for children. The stress values in the following tables for adults and for children bear an amazing similarity.

## THE HOLMS-RAHE STRESS TABLE FOR ADULTS

| LIFE EVENT | VALUE |
|---|---|
| 1. death of a spouse | 100 |
| 2. divorce | 73 |
| 3. marital separation | 65 |
| 4. jail term | 63 |
| 5. death of a close relative | 63 |
| 6. personal injury or illness | 53 |
| 7. marriage | 50 |
| 8. fired from job | 47 |
| 9. marital reconciliation | 45 |
| 10. retirement | 45 |
| 11. change in health of a family member | 44 |
| 12. pregnancy | 40 |
| 13. sex difficulties | 39 |
| 14. gain of new family member | 39 |
| 15. business readjustment | 39 |
| 16. change in financial state | 38 |
| 17. death of a close friend | 37 |
| 18. change to a different line of work | 36 |
| 19. change in number of arguments with spouse | 35 |
| 20. mortgage over $10,000 | 31 |

| | | |
|---|---|---|
| 21. | foreclosure of mortgage or loan | 30 |
| 22. | change in responsibilities at work | 29 |
| 23. | son or daughter leaving home | 29 |
| 24. | trouble with in-laws | 29 |
| 25. | outstanding personal achievement | 28 |
| 26. | wife begins or stops work | 26 |
| 27. | begin or end school | 26 |
| 28. | change in living conditions | 25 |
| 29. | revision of personal habits | 24 |
| 30. | trouble with boss | 23 |
| 31. | change in work hours or conditions | 20 |
| 32. | change in residence | 20 |
| 33. | change in schools | 20 |
| 34. | change in recreation | 19 |
| 35. | change in church activities | 19 |
| 36. | change in social activities | 18 |
| 37. | mortgage or loan less than $10,000 | 17 |
| 38. | change in sleeping habits | 16 |
| 39. | change in number of family get-togethers | 15 |
| 40. | change in eating habits | 15 |
| 41. | vacation | 13 |
| 42. | Christmas (or Hanukkah) | 12 |
| 43. | minor violations of the law | 11 |

| SCORE | STRESS POTENTIAL |
|---|---|
| 150–199 | moderate |
| 200–299 | medium |
| 300 or more | severe |

In the following table for children, not all events apply to all children, especially babies, who will be considered by themselves later.

# THE MILLER STRESS TABLE FOR CHILDREN

| LIFE EVENT | VALUE |
|---|---|
| 1. death of a parent | 100 |
| 2. divorce of parents | 73 |
| 3. separation of parents | 65 |
| 4. parent's jail term | 63 |
| 5. death of a close family member | 63 |
| 6. personal injury or illness | 53 |
| 7. parents' remarriage | 50 |
| 8. suspension or expulsion from school | 47 |
| 9. parents' reconciliation | 45 |
| 10. long vacation | 45 |
| 11. parent's or sibling's illness | 44 |
| 12. mother's pregnancy | 40 |
| 13. anxiety over sex | 39 |
| 14. birth of a sibling or adoption | 39 |
| 15. new school, classroom, or teacher | 39 |
| 16. money problems at home | 38 |
| 17. death or moving away of close friend | 37 |
| 18. change in studies | 36 |
| 19. more arguments with parent or parents arguing more | 35 |
| 20. not applicable for child | |
| 21. not applicable for child | |
| 22. change in school responsibilities | 29 |
| 23. sibling going away to school | 29 |
| 24. family arguments with grandparents | 29 |
| 25. winning school or community awards | 28 |
| 26. mother going to work or stopping work | 26 |
| 27. school beginning or ending | 26 |
| 28. family's standard of living changing | 25 |
| 29. change in personal habits, bedtime, homework, etc. | 24 |

| | | |
|---|---|---|
| 30. | trouble with parent, lack of communication, hostility, etc. | 23 |
| 31. | change in school hours, schedule of courses | 20 |
| 32. | family's moving | 20 |
| 33. | a new school | 20 |
| 34. | new sports, hobbies, family recreation activities | 19 |
| 35. | change in church activities | 19 |
| 36. | change in social activities, new friends, loss of old ones, peer pressures | 18 |
| 37. | not applicable for child | |
| 38. | change in sleeping habits | 16 |
| 39. | change in number of family get-togethers | 15 |
| 40. | change in eating habits, diets, etc. | 15 |
| 41. | vacation | 13 |
| 42. | Christmas (or Hanukkah) | 12 |
| 43. | breaking home, school, or church rules | 11 |

| SCORE | STRESS POTENTIAL |
|---|---|
| 150– 199 | moderate |
| 200– 299 | medium |
| 300 or more | severe |

The Holms-Rahe and the Mary Miller stress tables are reprinted from Mary Susan Miller, *Child Stress* (New York: Doubleday & Co., 1982). Reproduced with permission of the publisher.

Referring to this chart, you will see that a child can score moderate to severe stress very easily.

There are still more causes for childhood stress. Among them, fear is perhaps most common. Unlike adults, a child is not protected from fear by logic and reason. A child lives in an active fantasy world which, along with pleasant dreams, creates monsters that come lurking in the night searching for children to eat or kidnap. Shadows and sounds become creatures of the sea whose sole purpose in life is to frighten little people. Some children are easily frightened by strangers. Large animals, noisy appliances, and new fixtures in their environment also tend to make some children fearful. Other fears that possess children are of a more substantive nature. Abandonment is a fear that most children experience, if only for a short time. Separation, an event which takes place many times throughout life, is often to blame for this fear. Babies first have to face separation at birth. At that time, they leave the warm, secure environment where they have been developing for nine months to enter a world of loud noises, unfamiliar people, and other stimuli. Later, an infant learns that the mother who holds and comforts him will, at times, have to leave him. This is just the first of many separations that will help to install independence and autonomy in later childhood. But children will often experience a heightened sense of fear at these times of separation.

Children have still other fears to contend with. Those who are old enough to conceive such an occurrence are frightened by the possibility of nuclear war. According to Dr. Helen Caldicott, a Harvard University pediatrician who leads a worldwide organization of physicians concerned with nuclear arms issues, children are more frightened of war than are adults. Whereas adults have many defense mechanisms and denial systems that keep them thinking about other things, such as paying bills, seeking pleasure, and keeping their lives in order, children lack them. Instead, children are faced with the thought of their future being taken away from them by something they don't understand. They do understand that even their parents cannot save them from this night-mare. Dr. Caldicott, herself a parent, claims that much children's artwork is full of nuclear imagery and that their dreams are often filled with horrible scenes of war. Parents may have the luxury of being too busy to think of such disasters very often, but their children are faced with many unanswered questions and anxieties regarding war. Death, itself a mystery, also frightens them.

Television provides more fearsome material. From the time a child is born, television often serves as a daily companion. Children's programs depict cartoon characters blowing each other up with dynamite and guns, ramming their cars into walls, and finding other ways to startle young audiences to hold their attention. Other, more "realistic," programs offer scenes of murders, mug-gings, fires, and pillaging hour after hour. In between, the news brings violence even closer to home with current information and video coverage of the latest sensational crime. If babies are too young to grasp all this, they are nonetheless bombarded by frightening noises, screams, yells, and gunfire.

Parents can help their children relieve stress once they see the signals. There are many types of behavioral and physical disorders that reflect stress. Some children resort to destructive behavior. For example, one boy I know, three years of age, breaks his toys as well as his sister's toys and any china, glass, or other breakable object he can find. His baby sister receives much of his parents' attention, and that upsets him. In order to get the attention he craves he breaks everything in sight.

Some children frequently hurt themselves. A four-year-old girl I know is always falling or banging an arm or a leg. Crying, she runs to her mother or father to show them the new battle scars. This child is indeed fighting a battle. Her parents often argue at night and have little time for her during the day when they both work. She finds that by "hurting" herself she effectively gets her parents to notice her and care for her. In these cases, more parental attention, in the form of exercise and massage as shown in this book, would help answer the stress calls of children.

Still other children react with aggressive behavior. A friend has a four-year-old son who until recently did an excellent job of keeping visitors away. He lived with his parents and a single mother and daughter who was his age. The two children did not become friends. The girl was vocal and very aggressive. She received much attention for her negative behavior, causing the little boy, Jesse, to use aggressive acts to get similar attention. He became a formidable power, demanding his parents' attention by striking them or anyone else in his path. For several years, I visited his mother during preschool hours to avoid an encounter with little Jesse. Now four, Jesse is one of my best young friends. He is sensitive and intelligent, very generous with his toys as he is with his smiles. The change came about when his parents moved to their own house and away from the cause of his distress. They also made an effort to spend more time with him.

Some children, instead of aggressive or destructive behavior, will resort to apathy when under stress. Apathy is a way of tuning out the world when it becomes too painful. An apathetic child shows little healthy zest for life. Instead, he is listless and disinterested or simply bored. Children who are able to find sound outlets for their frustrations or fears often shed their apathy and become lively and happy. It should be clear to parents that although most children will exhibit signs of apathy now and then, chronic apathy is a sign that the child needs help.

Another form of coping with stress is excessive sleep. Sleep provides a nonfeeling time for children under stress. As adults we know how sleep on occasion serves as a solace when confronted by difficult tasks or painful emotional problems. Children, if they sleep for unusually long periods of time, may be seeking escape from their problems.

Psychosomatic illness or symptoms of a psychosomatic nature may be a result of stress. "Psychosomatic," in this case, means that the physical problem is in part due to the workings of the mind. According to Dr. Karl Menninger, "The stomach mirrors the emotions better than any other body system."[4] Rather than acting out their distress, many children develop stomach problems. Dr. William Liebman, writing in *Clinical Pediatrics*, reports that nearly 15 percent of all children suffer psychosomatic stomachaches, or stomachaches brought on in part by psychological means. He adds that as many as 44 percent of these children come from homes with marital or familial problems, while 30 percent experience pressure to achieve. These children's bodies house their feelings of distress in the form of varied digestive problems.[5]

Dr. Jonathan Kellerman, in his book *Helping the Fearful Child*, names anxiety, stomachaches, and asthma as stress symptoms in children. Psychologists would add chronic depression and mild forms of psychological disorders.

Certainly if a child's symptoms are severe, it would be advisable to seek professional help. If this is not the case, there is much that parents can do to ease the situation. To begin with, they can learn to identify their children's behavior and symptoms correctly. If the child is sending SOS signals, why is he or she doing so? By watching, observing, and talking to him, a parent may come to know the source of stress. Once parents understand why the child is stressed, they can offer help.

As mentioned, exercise and massage provide an effective way of dispelling stress. They have been used for centuries for this purpose, and we now have scientific evidence to explain their effectiveness. Athletes usually feel relaxed after a heavy workout, and scientists found that this is due to an increase in the production of hormones called endorphins. When received by the brain, endorphins produce a feeling of mild euphoria and an alert, relaxed

---

[4]Judy Dunn, *Distress and Comfort*, 54.

[5]William Liebman, "Recurrent Abdominal Pain in Children: A Retrospective Survey of 119 Patients." *Clinical Pediatrics* 17:2 (February 1978): 149–153.

state of mind. One does not have to be an athlete to experience this phenomenon.

Dr. Arthur S. Leon, an internationally known expert in the field of sports and medicine, names improved stress management as one of the important benefits of regular exercise. In addition to producing the endorphin effect, exercise stimulates nearly all the organs and systems of the body, improving their function. This greatly reduces the physical toll stress can take on the body. Perhaps our ancestors never suffered the cumulative effects of stress because they either had to run from or actively fight an aggressor, thereby relieving themselves of stress.

Doctors are now prescribing exercise in the treatment of mental illness due to stress. Dr. Keith Sehnert, in his book *Stress/Unstress*, cites the case study of Dr. John Greist, a psychiatrist who studied the effects of exercise on patients with severe depression. His 1976 pilot study demonstrates that exercise can be more effective than psychotherapy. Eight patients were enrolled in a ten-week program that included jogging two to seven times a week alone and in groups. After ten weeks, six of the patients were cured.[6]

Researchers at the National Institutes of Health have recently found that massage and other "hands-on" treatments increase the production of endorphins, the same hormones found in higher concentration in people who exercise. This seems to account for the tranquility enjoyed by children and adults after they have been massaged.

My father is an example of someone who learned the joy of exercise from an early age. As a young boy growing up in Europe he swam, hiked, and bicycled throughout childhood. Now in his late fifties, my father is an avid bicyclist, cycling a distance of fifty miles to work each day. When asked what he does to relax, he just smiles. Driving to work produces stress, he claims, whereas his bicycle commute of an hour and twenty minutes relieves stress after a day's work.

A young friend of seven returned home from a rough day at school. "Mom, I've had a hard day," he said as he wiped imaginary sweat off his brow. "My teacher made me eat my apple after my pizza and I didn't want to. She made me eat it anyway. Boy, am I mad! I'm going to get on my bicycle,

---

[6]Keith W. Sehnert, M.D., *Stress/Unstress* (Minneapolis: Augsburg Publishing House, 1981), 172–173.

let the wind blow through my hair and feel the sun on my back. See ya', Mom." He ran out the door to find his bike. He certainly knew how to relieve his stress!

Jasmine is a beautiful four-year-old girl. With her sunny disposition and her lovely smile, she is a joy to see and to play with. Jasmine has received massage and exercise from her mother, a physical therapist, since birth. She seems to know intuitively when she needs to be held or massaged. At times, if she is upset, she will run outside, telling her mother that she will be nicer when she returns from exercising. Jasmine is one of the most independent, relaxed, and happy children I know.

As a family activity, massage and exercise can relieve stress on a broader level. Stress often becomes a pattern in family life. The moods and temperaments of different family members may cause disputes and arguments. At these times an exercise break can be especially helpful. A woman I know finds her running shoes mysteriously placed by her door whenever she is giving her children a hard time. They have come to realize that Mommy is nicer after a run. Another friend often receives a back massage from his six-year-old son when he returns from work. He tells me that this has helped him to be a better father, more relaxed and easygoing in the evenings.

I think you will find, as have many parents, that massage and exercise as taught in this book will help answer the stress signals your child or baby may be sending. Responding to these signals as they arise, you can help reduce or prevent the cumulative effects of stress. Children can then learn from an early age how best to cope with stress for better health and well-being. It is true that we live in difficult times. Yet our response to stress can make the difference between health and illness, between happiness and depression.

# 5

# Passages

When you closely observe the first years of an infant and child, you witness the beautiful unfolding of human life. From a seemingly helpless state at birth, the infant grows and matures to become a fully capable child. During the first few years, growth and development progress very rapidly. According to Dr. Burton White, "Good child rearing in the initial stages of a baby's life includes knowing what the normal pattern of emerging skills is and facilitating their emergence."

The massage and exercise programs in this book should help parents encourage the development of their children. This chapter shows you exactly how these programs benefit a child's development.

## THE FIRST TWO MONTHS

In the initial two months of a baby's life the newborn will be less able to care for himself (or herself) than at any other time. His needs will be simple. First he will need to be fed and kept warm and clean. He will also be in need of cuddling and stroking to help make the transition into his world as gentle as possible. His need for contact during this time will help secure the bond between him and his parents.

The newborn baby will exhibit many reflex movements which are the precursors to later development. Many of these reflexes are present at birth to ensure his survival. For instance, the rooting reflex causes the baby to turn his head toward anything touched to his cheek, to find the nipple of his mother's breast or his bottle and begin sucking. This reflex provides the infant with effective feeding behavior.

The massage program during this stage is useful in making the baby feel more comfortable. If the birth has been traumatic, massage will help soothe the newborn. Very little pressure is used in this initial stage. Parents will also want to stay away from the navel until it is fully healed. Massage during this period is a way of telling the baby that he is loved and cherished, safe and secure.

The exercise program is of a passive nature at this time. The baby, having been tightly confined for many months before being born, will often show signs of delight at having his arms and legs stretched and moved.

Massage and exercise used within the first few months of life will help quiet the baby. Colic, a common affliction of infants, can often be relieved with these methods.

## TWO TO FOUR MONTHS

The infant who had been interested only in being fed, clothed, held, and kept warm and dry evolves in this stage into a baby who begins to take an interest in the world around him. His longer wakeful periods reflect this. Although he is still unable to move about very much, he does exhibit greater body and head control. During this period, the reflexlike behavior seen in the preceding months begins to disappear. Instead, your baby's movement will be somewhat more defined. He will seem to have greater strength and will want to use it. The three-month-old baby will often take pleasure in kicking any surface that provides pressure to the soles of the feet. He generally takes great interest in his body.

The massage program will be useful in quieting the baby and comforting him when he encounters difficulties. The baby's body is beginning to awaken now with new and different kinds of movement and skills. Massage can be helpful both in encouraging this awakening and in soothing muscles that are beginning to work for the first time.

Exercise will also enhance this development. Still passive, the exercise program will nonetheless be helpful in encouraging movement. It will help to strengthen and stretch his muscles as well as to relax them. The exercises will also help to give full rotation to the joints.

The baby will especially enjoy the arm exercises, which allow for full range of motion while stretching and toning the arms. With the "sole press" exercise, the baby will greatly enjoy kicking against your hands.

During this period, the massage and exercise programs make the most of your baby's interests and developing skills. He will watch the face of the person massaging or exercising him with great interest, and he will enjoy the physical contact. The pleasure he derives from these activities should encourage parents to practice them regularly.

## FOUR TO EIGHT MONTHS

This stage of infancy is a period punctuated by broader interests and acquisition of new skills, including turning over, crawling, and sitting. The infant is now taking more and more interest in faces, voices, and nearly everything close to him. This is the last period during which he observes the world from a horizontal position, and he seems to want to make the most of it. The beginning of sensorimotor skills, such as visual-directed reaching or hand-eye coordination, can be observed in an infant during this stage.

He is also more able and more adept at using his muscles, reaching for objects, and hearing and seeing the world around him with greater sensitivity. It is almost as though his curiosity is being primed for the time when he will be able to move about and satisfy his interests in his surroundings. He will begin to practice turning from front to back to front again, and will achieve a sitting position unaided.

The massage program during this time will be helpful in relaxing him when fatigued. Massage will relieve tired muscles and other discomforts. Exercise will serve to stimulate muscle use, especially in the large leg muscles, abdominal muscles, and arms. These exercises will help make the transition into the walking stage an easier one. Similarly the back exercise will be useful in establishing strength needed for sitting and walking.

## EIGHT TO TWELVE MONTHS

The baby now enters a very important stage of development. The kind of experience he or she has during this period will help to shape his personality, his language and social development, and his intelligence. Motor development will accelerate during this period as the child begins to walk. This is a time of active exploration of the world, and babies at this age tend to be very curious. The baby will begin to master many of the skills that were developed in preceding months, and these will help him in his explorations.

At this time, he will benefit greatly from having regular massage. It will help calm him and ease him through the complex movements involved in standing and walking.

The exercise program at this stage will help facilitate his new endeavors. Your baby will develop strength through exercise, which will help him to stand and walk unaided. By exercising he will learn how to tighten his leg muscles and to stand erect, and he will also learn to balance himself and use his muscles to support himself. The exercise program during this time will be useful in helping to develop overall strength and flexibility.

## THE ONE-YEAR OLD

A child at this stage will be leaving babyhood behind. He will begin to exhibit more of his own personality, his strength, and his abilities. Development of language, social, intellectual, and motor skills will continue at a rapid rate.

The massage program during this period will serve to soothe him when he is cranky or tired. It may also be helpful at bedtime. Massage at this age can be used after the exercise program or at any other time of the day to help him relax.

The exercise program for this age period takes into consideration the new motor development and the increasing strength and agility of the toddler. Whereas the exercises were mostly passive before, they now involve the child and require his or her active participation. The arm exercises will help develop the arm muscles and torso. They will also serve to encourage coordination. It is important at this stage to let the child do as much as he can by himself in executing the exercises. After he learns a pattern, he may initiate the exercises himself when you sit down together. The arm exercises are also helpful in stimulating heart and lung activity, and for encouraging full rotation of the shoulder joints.

The abdominal exercises will make use of the muscles of the torso, which are needed for such activities as walking, climbing, and sitting. By strengthening these muscles, such activities will be easier for him to do.

The leg exercises involve the toddler's strongest muscles. The "leg stretch" both stretches and strengthens the quadraceps and inner thigh muscles while encouraging full rotation in the hip joint. The "butterfly" exercise also rotates the hip joint, but in another way.

The "scissors" exercise is good for coordination. It also stretches the legs very gently. The "happy feet" exercise is excellent for promoting flexibility in the ankle and the Achilles tendon. The "jack-in-the-box" makes use of leg muscles, torso, and arms. The "bridge," which strengthens the back muscles, is followed by the forward bend, which relaxes them and extends the back in the opposite way.

The one-year-old will probably want to take a good deal of initiative with this program. Let him do as much as possible.

## THE TWO- AND THREE-YEAR-OLD

The child of two to four years is probably going to keep his parents quite busy. He seems to have boundless energy and a full capacity to enjoy and further develop new skills. Climbing and running seem to be the choice activities of this child, and even a parent who jogs three miles a day may have difficulty keeping up. He exhibits a zest for life, developing his personality, intelligence, and social skills while increasing his motor development.

This child also seems to lack control of his body as he races around, climbs anything that can possibly be climbed, and flings himself from one activity into another. He has well-developed gross motor skills, but sensorimotor skills have yet to be mastered.

Preceding exercise programs helped new skills and abilities emerge. The program for this stage continues to do this while helping the child master and refine these skills. Exercise now serves to develop greater strength, agility, coordination, and flexibility.

The warm-up serves to ready the cardiovascular system and the muscles for exercise. It protects the muscles from being overworked too quickly. The aerobic exercises further stimulate the heart and lungs. Daily use of these exercises will help develop the cardiovascular system.

The arm exercises help to strengthen the arm muscles, while fully rotating the shoulder joints. These exercises alternately flex and extend the arm muscles, contributing to full development.

50

The torso exercises work the abdominal muscles to strengthen them. The leg exercises work all the major muscles of the legs, helping to both strengthen and increase flexibility. The remaining exercises for the back help to increase flexibility and gently strengthen the back.

The massage program will be useful at this time, as it has been during other periods, to soothe and quiet the child. Massage will also help ease some of the child's tense moments and will be effective in relieving muscle soreness due to growing pains or exercise.

## THE FOUR- AND FIVE-YEAR-OLD

At this stage, we find a child who is well poised and less extreme in his (or her) activities and movements. His skills are more refined. He becomes adept at using his play equipment. Hand-eye coordination has advanced. Your child takes great pleasure in utilizing his newfound skills and abilities. Exercise during this period will help increase the child's agility and strength while enabling him to refine his small motor functions.

The massage program used now will help the child relax at bedtime or at any time that he is frustrated, anxious, or moody. The entire massage program for this age group may be used at any time.

The exercise program is now longer, and it should provide a healthy outlook for the exuberant child. The warm-up exercises assume greater importance so as to ready the child for more intensive exercise. The aerobic exercises stimulate the cardiovascular system. Used regularly, they will help to strengthen heart and lung action. The last exercise in the aerobic section is a cool-down exercise to help the heart and lung rate return to normal. It is also an excellent stretching exercise for the hamstring muscles.

The arm exercises stretch and strengthen the major muscles in the growing arms, providing the child with greater muscle control. These exercises also strengthen the torso and chest. The torso exercises help to strengthen the abdominal muscles as well as the arms. In the leg exercise section, the child will have greater opportunity to develop leg muscles while gaining more control over movement as well. These exercises are demanding, but enjoyable, for most children.

The increasing physical activities of a child of this age necessarily make increasing demands on his back. It now becomes more important than ever to strengthen the back so as to avert the lower back problems that often develop as a result of the sedentary, urban life so many of us are destined to lead. The back exercises for this age group are designed to help achieve this purpose.

By gradually strengthening and relaxing the muscular and cardiovascular systems of your child as he or she grows from one stage to another, the exercise and massage programs should make an important contribution toward a healthier and happier life in later years.

## QUALITY TIME

Time for most people is a precious commodity. Although advanced technology continues to devise ways of saving us time, most of us are still craving more hours in the day to do what we need and want to do. For parents, the time squeeze is usually far greater than it is for others. Many parents find that keeping house, tending their careers, and raising children leave them with few free moments.

Adding to the pressure, children are in dire need of their parents' time. They need to feel the warmth of their parents' touch. They require their parents' involvement, especially during their formative years, to ensure their healthy growth and development. It is important too that they receive their parents' attention simply to be reassured that they are loved and cherished.

Parents are often hard pressed to find the time to give children their full attention. Children have to be sent off to school. Meals have to be cooked. The myriad chores and responsibilities of modern life leave very little time for simply enjoying one another's company. Children find ways of expressing their need for attention. Some cry or throw tantrums. Others break things, and still others become withdrawn. To solve this problem, it's important to make the very best use of whatever time is available.

Although many families may have little time to spend together, this does not have to handicap their relationship. In *Distress and Comfort*, Judy Dunn cites studies performed in Israel on the agricultural communes, or *kibbutzim*. There, children are cared for during the day in small groups by a *metapelet*, or caretaker. In the evenings, children are brought to their parents' houses where they may spend two hours with them. Although the children spend eight to ten hours each day with their *metapelets* and only two hours with their parents each evening, their attachments to their parents were found to be as intense and strong as those of American children for their parents. Judy Dunn feels that this is due to the "loving and intense interaction" children have with their parents each evening.[1]

By spending even half an hour a day with your child, giving him your full, undivided attention, you can achieve quality time. The massage and exercise programs in this book provide an excellent means of achieving quality time with your child. These activities provide parents and children with time together spent thoroughly enjoying one another. They allow for much contact, laughter, and play, while providing tools for development and growth. They should contribute to making children more responsive and less distressed.

A couple I know had their first daughter recently. Both are lawyers and spend long hours in offices and in court before coming home to Jessica. Jessica's mother complained to me that she felt guilty and depressed over not having more time to spend with her daughter. Her husband voiced the same concerns. I introduced them to massage and exercise programs, which they began using for their daughter in the evening and on weekends. They now tell me that they have come much closer to Jessica since acquiring quality time through exercise and massage.

I believe that you, too, will find these programs to be helpful in making the most of whatever time you have to spend with your children.

[1]Judy Dunn, *Distress and Comfort* (Cambridge: Harvard University Press, 1977), 64.

# II

# Exercise Program

# 6

# Getting Ready for Exercise

Before starting the exercise program, there are a few simple preparations and a few points you might keep in mind.

The program has been structured so that you will need little more than yourself, your child, your attention to the illustrated directions, and your enthusiasm. You can manage quite well with what you have available to you. It will not be necessary to buy special exercise equipment or exercise clothing. And you won't have to build a special exercise area. A few square feet even in the smallest apartment will do. A firm mattress or a towel, carpet, or blanket on the floor will provide the necessary cushioning.

Be sure the room is warm—but not too warm—and that there are no drafts. When exercising outdoors, it should not be too hot or too cool.

As for clothing: your baby might wear a diaper, a loose fitting gown, or nothing at all. If your baby is exercised in the nude, be prepared for sudden showers! Change your baby before exercising so that he or she won't be uncomfortable.

Clothing for you and your older child should be comfortable and loose. If you prefer, you might wear leotards or warm-up suits. However, there is a drawback to special clothing. Sporting goods merchants have encouraged the idea that special clothing is necessary for exercise. And when adults do not have it, they have an excuse for not exercising. We adults have enough excuses for dodging exercise without passing this one on to our children. I suggest you impress on your child that he can exercise perfectly well without any special clothing.

When your baby is older, you will need a little more space to move as you exercise. Make sure that you have some padding on the floor—a mat, towel, carpet, or blanket will do. An area of about four square feet should be enough for exercising your toddler.

For your older child, eligible for Group III and Group IV exercises (ages two through five), you will require a slightly larger area because the programs become more active. Six square feet should be more than enough. Select an area in your home that is free of breakable objects and sharp corners on furniture. When exercising outdoors, you might wear sneakers to protect your feet from broken glass, nails, or other unpleasant surprises.

It may be helpful to establish a regular time and place for exercise. This will enable you to create both a routine and a habit. These will make exercise a regular part of daily living—as important and valuable as eating and sleeping. The time of day when your baby is most alert and full of energy will usually be the best time for exercise. It is advisable not to exercise just after a meal. Allow at least thirty minutes after feeding before exercising your baby. In the case of older children, you might choose a time that best fits your schedule. And once you establish a suitable time, it would be best to stick to it and not keep moving it around.

When children are unwell or uncooperative, it will be necessary, of course, to cancel the exercise period. As mentioned earlier, a parent should never force exercise upon a child—at any age. Exercise should be a voluntary and pleasurable activity. In most cases, children will find exercise fun, and they will look forward to their daily exercise program. From time to time, when it is necessary to suspend the program, the chances are that your child will soon be ready and eager to resume it.

The exercises of the first two groups, up to your child's second birthday, are to be handled by either or both parents with care. There should be no abrupt movements at any time in stretching and relaxing the muscles of your infant's arms, legs, neck, and back. Though an infant is born with far greater strength than most of us give him credit for, joints and muscles are still relatively weak. This should always be kept in mind, especially since there is a tendency on the part of some parents to become overconfident as the child displays increasing strength, self-assurance, familiarity, and pleasure with the exercises. Furthermore, an abrupt movement is inadvisable at any time and at any age. During the first year, be sure to note those exercises not recommended for the newborn.

Another important point to be kept in mind, especially during your child's first two years: never force the exercises on your infant or force the pace of your child's development. Exercise must have the acceptance and consent of the child. If your baby is not in the mood, is not interested, or becomes bored, then suspend the exercises. He or she might be more responsive if you switch to a few massage strokes. You can return to the exercise program at a more favorable time.

You should always remember that exercise is meant to be pleasurable. Any hint of force or of running against a child's will is almost certain to produce trouble rather than pleasure. And the parent should also bear in mind that the purpose of exercise is to promote not only physical but also the psychological and emotional development. These purposes unquestionably are best served in an environment of pleasure and fun. When exercise becomes enjoyable it can become a welcome lifelong routine and a lifelong source of preventive health care—one which may reduce future medical and hospital bills by thousands and perhaps hundreds of thousands of dollars.

You should follow the exercises in the order they appear. This will give your child a well-balanced workout. It is also advisable that you complete each program from start to finish so as to secure the maximum benefit from the daily session. Should it be necessary to interrupt the series of exercises, then I would suggest that you complete the routine as soon as you can.

You may have begun talking to your baby from birth, and you would be well advised to continue talking to him or to her during the exercise routine. Your baby may not understand the words, but he may very well begin to sense your mood and even your meaning. Eventually, of course, he will learn the language from you and the others who speak to him.

Music has proved to be another valuable accompaniment to exercise for children and adults of all ages. It provides a rhythm to which the exercises can be keyed. Its melody and harmony contribute to creating the pleasant environment that is so desirable for exercise. Select the music that appeals to your ears and those of your child.

When your child is old enough to understand, you might tell him something about his muscles. Many children and adults "exercise" without really exercising. Here is an example that you and your child can both use:

Raise your right arm in the air. Now bring it down by your side. What did you feel? Now raise your right arm again, but this time stretch it as high and as far as you can, as if trying to reach the ceiling or the sky. This time did you feel the muscles tighten down your right side and did you feel your fingers stretching? These are the sensations of muscles at work. And that is exercise!

Ask your child what he feels as he does a sit-up. Does he feel his stomach muscles working? When you do a leg lift, let him feel one of your muscles popping up. Explanations and illustrations of this kind will help show your child what is happening when he exercises his body.

When first exercising your muscles, you and your child may feel some soreness. This is to be expected. It indicates that your muscles are rusty. Bathing in warm water will help soothe a sore muscle. In a short time, after regular exercise, the soreness will disappear.

How long should you exercise your child? That depends on several factors: your child's age group, his strength, and the rate of his development. In general, the following will serve as guidelines:

Group I for infants up to one year of age: ten minutes, once or twice daily
Group II for babies from one to two years: fifteen minutes, once or twice daily
Group III for children from two to three years: twenty minutes, once or twice daily
Group IV for children from three through five years of age: thirty minutes, once or twice daily

When you find your child comfortable and accomplished with a series of exercises, you may want to consider repeating the program later in the day. Exercises twice daily, if agreeable to your child, may be highly beneficial.

In starting a program, use the recommended number of repetitions for each exercise. If your child can handle more repetitions, encourage him to do so and increase the overall exercise time accordingly.

Some children advance more rapidly than others. It is advisable to let your child proceed at his own comfortable pace, encouraging him at the same time to make an effort to extend his strength a bit more each day. If you find that he has acquired sufficient strength and agility, you may want to consider moving him ahead into the next exercise group, even though he has not reached the age period for that group. That would be the equivalent of skipping a class in school.

On the other hand, if your child is proceeding slowly, you might keep him in his group of exercises even after he is scheduled to move on to the next group. There is no need to rush him. In time he will acquire the strength and agility to catch up.

Whatever the rate at which your child proceeds, it is important, as often mentioned, that he exercise regularly and daily, without interruption if that is at all possible. If you make exercise a daily habit, you and your child won't have to expend energy thinking about it. You will simply do it as a matter of course. But there is another important reason for exercising on a daily basis. The nature of exercise is such that it builds upon itself from one day to the next. And as exercise proceeds on a regular basis, the muscles and the cardiovascular system of the body gather momentum in building strength. If you and your child begin to falter in carrying out the daily routine, the strength you have built up in your bodies will begin to lessen. You will lose momentum, and soon you will be right back to where you started, losing time as well as energy.

If you and your child are running, swimming, or engaging in some sport, by all means continue doing so. There should be no conflict with the exercise program in this book. These programs will enhance your sport activity, provide a balanced routine, and probably reach muscles that are bypassed by other activity.

A final suggestion: vacation time is a great time for exercise. Before setting out on a long drive, you may find it useful to exercise with your child. This will release excess energy, put him in a more pleasant and calm mood, and turn him into a much better traveling companion. As the benefits of exercise wane, you may find it useful to break up the monotony of a long ride by repeating the exercise routine. All you need to take along with you in the car is a copy of the book of exercises, if you haven't already memorized them.

And all you now need to initiate the exercise program is to turn to the one that fits the age of your child.

# 7

# The First Twelve Months

# GROUP I EXERCISES

## *Arms*

Purpose: to stretch and relax your baby's arms and upper body and to encourage muscle development and flexibility in the arms and upper body.

## ONE: HUGGING
### Repeat five times.

Position: your baby lies on his back on a firm mattress, carpet, towel, or on your legs.

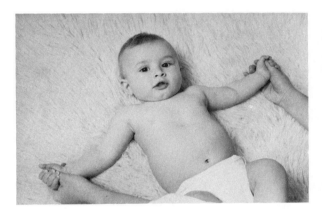

1. Take your baby's hands, letting him grasp yours, and bring arms out to his sides forming a letter *T*.

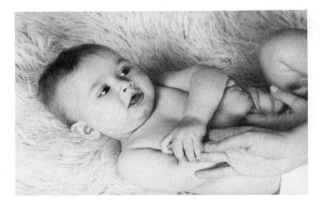

2. Now, bring your baby's arms across his chest into a hug.

3. Repeat by bringing the arms out to the sides and then hug reversing arm positions.

NOTE: Never pull hard on your baby's arms. Gently move them instead.

## TWO: SCISSORS
### Repeat five times.

Position: same as for previous exercise.

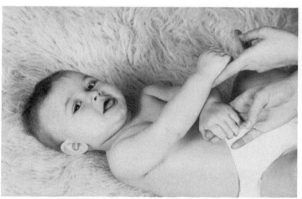

1. Continue holding your baby's hands. Bringing your baby's arms toward you, crisscross them at the wrist.

2. Now, crisscross them reversing the position of the arms.

NOTE: Six weeks of age and up.

# THREE: SIDE STRETCH
### Repeat five times.

Position: same as for previous exercise.

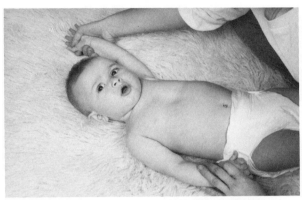

1. Continue holding your baby's hands. Bring one arm up over and along your baby's head while you bring the other arm down and alongside his hip.

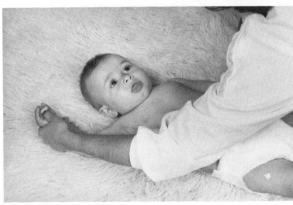

2. Reverse positions of the arms bringing them up as you do so.

NOTE: Move your baby's arms very gently. Do not pull the arms quickly or hard.

# FOUR: CHEST STRETCH
### Repeat five times.

Position: same as for previous exercise.

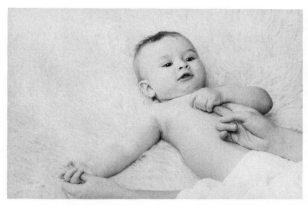

1. Continue holding your baby's arms; gently extend one arm out to the side while bringing the other arm to baby's chest.

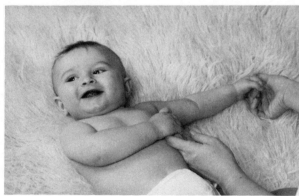

2. Reverse the position of the arms.

# *Torso*

Purpose: to encourage muscle development of the torso.

## ONE: PULL-UPS
Repeat five times.

Position: your baby lies on your outstretched legs, feet pointing toward you.

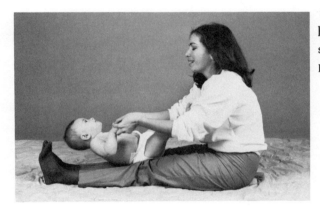

1. Let your baby grasp your hands as you gently and slowly pull him to a sitting position.

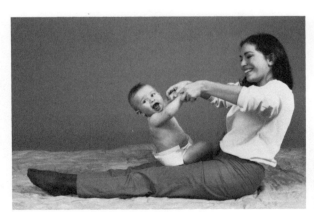

2. Now let your baby down again slowly onto your legs.

NOTE: Use after six weeks of age or when your baby has head control.

# *Legs*

Purpose: to encourage muscle development of the legs and to stretch and relax legs, muscles, and feet; to encourage flexibility in the knee, hip, and ankle joints.

## ONE: KNEE-CHEST STRETCH
### Repeat five times.

Position: your baby lies in front of you on his back or on your outstretched legs.

1. Holding your baby's feet, gently bring his knees to his chest.

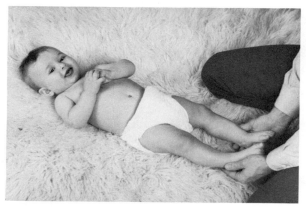

2. Now bring your baby's legs straight out on the pad or your legs.

# TWO: MARCHING
### Repeat five times.

Position: same as for previous exercise.

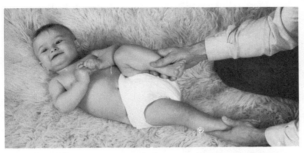

1. Holding your baby's feet or calves, bring one knee to his chest while you straighten the other leg.

2. Alternate, bringing the other knee in.

# THREE: SOLE PRESS
### Press five to ten times.

Position: same as for previous exercise.

Bring knees over your baby's chest; place your hands on baby's feet and press gently, encouraging a kicking response. Continue as long as your baby kicks.

# FOUR: INNER THIGH STRETCH
Repeat five times.

Position: same as for previous exercise.

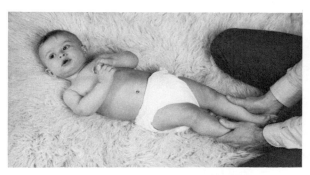

1. Holding your baby's feet, bring legs straight toward you, side by side.

2. Gently separate legs to form a letter *V*.

# FIVE: HAPPY FEET
Repeat three times each foot.

Position: same as for previous exercise.

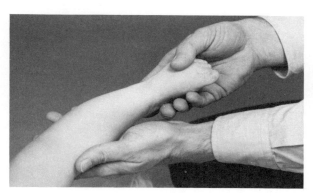

1. Take your baby's foot in your hands. Holding foot at the calf with one hand, gently press your baby's foot to point toes, using the thumb and fingers of your other hand. Hold for five seconds.

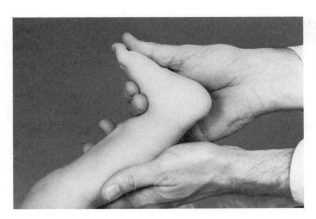

2. Gently flex your baby's foot, using your thumb to press it back, bending it at the ankle.

# Back

Purpose: to encourage flexibility and muscle development of the back.

## ONE: ARCH
Repeat three times.

Position: lie on your back with your baby lying facing you on your stomach.

1. Hold your baby's hands and lift his upper body up off your stomach.

2. Bring your baby back down to your stomach.

NOTE: Use after six weeks of age.

73

# 8

# The One- to Two-Year-Olds

# GROUP II EXERCISES

## *Arms*

Purpose:   to increase strength in the arms and upper body. To stimulate the cardiovascular system and help develop coordination.

### ONE: BOXING
Repeat five times.

Position: sit with your child facing you.

1. Hold hands with your child, bringing one arm forward and the other arm back, bending at the elbow.

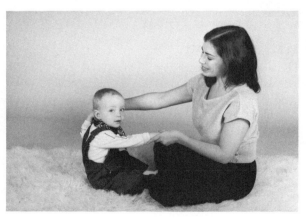

2. Now bring the opposite arm forward as you bring the other arm back.

## TWO: SWINGING
Repeat five times.

Position: same as for previous exercise.

1. Bring your child's arms to the starting position.

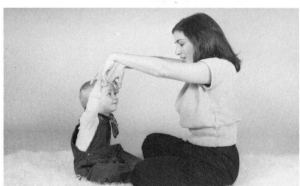

2. Hold hands with your child and stretch them out to the side, then up over his head.

## THREE: TWIST
Repeat five times.

Position: same as for previous exercise.

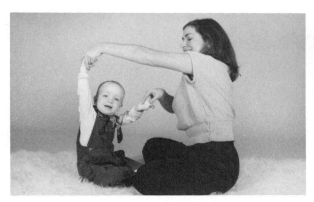

1. Take your child's hands and raise his arms over his head. Twist upper body to the right.

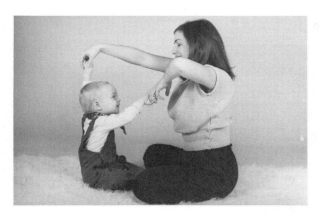

2. Now twist to the left.

# FOUR: SCISSORS
### Repeat ten times.

Position: same as for previous exercise.

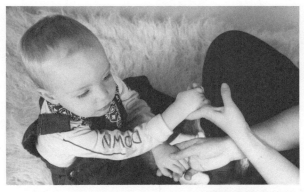

1. Continue to hold hands with your child. With his arms straight in front of him, crisscross his arms at the wrist.

2. Now crisscross the other way reversing the arm position.

79

## *Torso*

Purpose:   to strengthen abdominal and arm muscles.

## ONE: PULL-UPS
Repeat five to ten times.

Position: sit with your child lying between your outstretched legs.

1. Hold hands and slowly pull your child up to a sitting position letting him use his arm and stomach muscles as much as possible.

2. Now slowly lower your child back to the floor between your legs.

# TWO: ROCKING HORSE
### Repeat five times.

Position: sit as before with your child sitting, legs outstretched, between your outstretched legs.

1. Hold hands with your child, pulling him forward toward you.

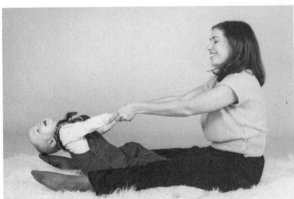

2. Now let him lean back as far as possible without touching his head to the floor. Encourage him to arch his back.

# Legs

Purpose: to encourage muscle development and flexibility in the legs. To help develop coordination.

## ONE: ALTERNATING LEG STRETCH
### Repeat five times.

Position: your child lies on his back with you sitting at his feet.

1. Holding your child's leg at the calf or ankle, bring one knee to his chest, keeping other leg straight.

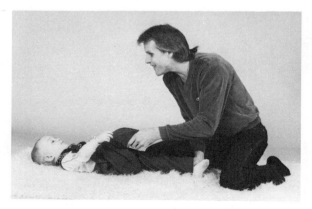

2. Alternate, bringing the other knee to the chest while keeping the first leg straight.

## TWO: SCISSORS
Repeat ten times.

Position: same as for previous exercise.

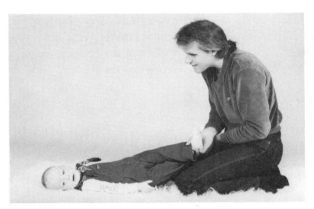

1. Take your child's feet and cross them at the ankle. Keep the legs close to the floor.

2. Now crisscross the other way.

## THREE: BUTTERFLY
Repeat five times.

Position: same as for previous exercise.

1. Bend your child's legs bringing the knees together, feet flat on the floor.

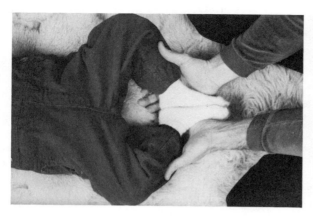

2. Now move knees apart toward the floor keeping the feet together. *Do not force* the legs any farther than they will go easily. Little by little your child's legs will become more flexible at the hip joint, allowing the knees to come closer to the floor.

## FOUR: HAPPY FEET
Repeat four times.

Position: same as for previous exercise.

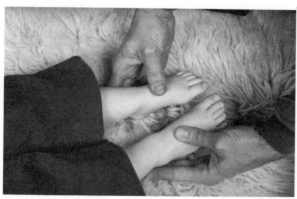

1. Take your child's feet. Using your thumbs, gently press down, pointing toes toward the floor. Press only as far as they will go easily.

2. Now use your thumbs under the feet to flex the feet back gently, bending at the ankles. Again, only flex as far as the feet will go easily.

# FIVE: JACK-IN-THE-BOX
Repeat three to five times.

Position: sit with your child sitting facing you.

1. Hold hands and stretch your child's arms high above his head, leaning him forward.

3. Now pull your child all the way up into a standing position, arms up in the air.

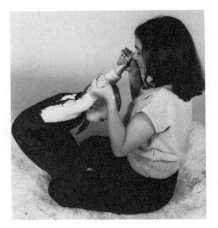

2. Stretching his arms even farther, encourage him to straighten his legs so that he is bending forward at the waist; legs straight.

NOTE: At first, you may be helping your child considerably; as your child progresses, he will use his muscles more and more. Encourage him to do so.

# Back

Purpose:   to strengthen the back and encourage flexibility.

## ONE: BRIDGE
Repeat three times.

Position: your child lies on his back with his knees bent, feet flat on floor.

1. Holding your child at the waist, help him to raise his torso up off the floor, encouraging him to use his leg and buttocks muscles. Hold for a few seconds.

2. Now lower him back to the floor keeping his knees bent.

# TWO: FORWARD BEND
## Repeat five times.

Position: your child sits on your lap or just in front of you.

1. Hold hands and bring your child's arms straight above his head.

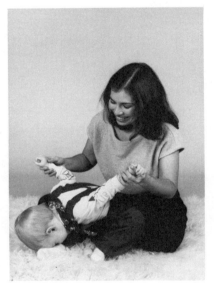

3. Allow your child to bend all the way over, touching the floor if he can, while you support him holding his arms up behind him.

2. Now keeping his arms a little behind him, help him to bend over.

# 9

# The Two- to Three-Year-Olds

# GROUP III EXERCISES

## *Warm-up*

Purpose: to ready the muscles for exercise, stimulate the cardiovascular system, and stretch.

## ONE: SWAYING
### Repeat five times.

Position: stand with your child in front of you, facing forward.

1. Take your child's hands, bringing them up over her head. Sway her arms to one side as she bends a little at the waist.

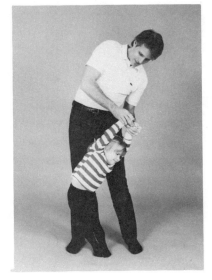

2. Sway her arms to the other side, letting her bend now to that side.

# TWO: AIRPLANE
### Repeat five times.

Position: stand with your child.

1. You and your child lace fingers behind your necks with elbows outstretched. Continue to face forward as you bend to one side.

2. Now bend to the other side.

# THREE: KICKING
Repeat five times.

Position: standing.

1. Hold hands with your child facing the same direction. Kick one leg out in front.

2. Now kick the other leg out.

93

## *Aerobics*

Purpose: to stimulate the cardiovascular system, building endurance and coordination.

### ONE: JUMP AND RUN
One to five minutes.

Position: stand facing each other.

1. Join hands and jump together.

2. Continue to hold hands and run in place. (March if your child can't run in place.)

# TWO: JUMPING JACKS
### Repeat five times.

Position: stand facing each other holding hands.

1. Jump, landing with feet apart.

2. Jump again, landing with feet together.

## Arms

Purpose: to strengthen and improve flexibility in the arms and upper body and to improve coordination.

### ONE: WINGS
Repeat five times.

Position: sit with your child facing you between your outstretched legs.

1. Begin with arms down at your sides.

2. Raise arms over head and stretch. Bring arms back down to your sides.

# TWO: CLIMB ROPE
### Repeat five times.

Position: same as for previous exercise.

1. Leaving one arm at your side, reach other arm up above your head and stretch, bending to the side very slightly.

2. Lower arm and stretch other arm over head.

NOTE: To make sure you are stretching enough, reach your opposite arm around and feel the muscles at your waist when you are reaching with the other arm. These muscles should feel hard.

## THREE: FISTS AND FINGERS
Repeat ten times.

Position: same as for previous exercise.

1. With arms outstretched, make fists and move your arms together and apart very quickly, fluttering them only an inch or two back and forth.

2. Keeping same position, stretch fingers apart and repeat fluttering movement.

## FOUR: ARM CIRCLES
Make ten circles each forward and backward.

Position: same as for previous exercise.

1. Stretch your arms to the sides and make fists.

2. Make small circles with your arms first forward, then backward.

# FIVE: HUGGING
Repeat ten times.

Position: same as for previous exercise.

1. Bring your arms tightly around your chest in a hug.

2. Repeat, changing arm positions.

## Torso

Purpose: to strengthen the torso and stretch the hamstrings.

### ONE: SALUTE
Repeat five times.

Position: both of you sit with your legs open wide, your child's toes touching inside your legs.

1. Hands behind your neck, elbows out to the side, sit tall and straight.

2. Bend at the waist, bringing heads toward the floor. Now slowly pull yourselves up to a sitting position.

# TWO: SEE-SAW
Repeat ten times.

Position: sit with your child facing you between your outstretched legs.

1. Join hands and lean forward while your child leans back.

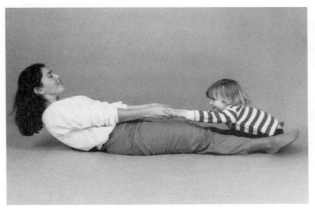

2. Now reverse positions, leaning back while your child leans forward.

## Legs

Purpose: to strengthen and stretch the legs and abdominal muscles and to improve coordination.

### ONE: LEG LIFTS
Repeat five times.

Position: sit with your legs open wide, your child between your legs facing away from you.

1. With your hands behind you for support, lift one leg, then lower.

2. Repeat with other leg.

### TWO: HAPPY FEET
Repeat five times.

Position: same as for previous exercise.

1. Point your toes as much as you can.

2. Now flex your feet, bending at the ankle.

# THREE: KNEE STRETCH
Repeat five times.

Position: sit side by side, legs straight out, hands behind hips.

1. Bring one knee up to your chest, keeping the other leg on the floor.

2. Alternate, bringing other knee to the chest.

# FOUR: DOUBLE KNEE STRETCH
### Repeat five times.

Position: same as for previous exercise.

1. Bring both knees to your chest.

2. Lower slowly back to the floor.

# FIVE: LEG LIFTS
### Repeat five times.

Position: lie on your side facing each other.

1. Raise up on your elbows for support. Lift your upper leg as high as you can, then lower. Repeat five times.

2. Change sides and repeat five times with your other leg.

# *Back*

Purpose: to increase strength and flexibility in the back.

## ONE: WINDMILL
### Repeat five times.

Position: sit with your child between your opened legs, each of you facing the same direction.

1. Take hands and bend your child over to one side stretching one arm up and over the head and the other arm down like a windmill.

2. Bend to the other side reversing arms.

## TWO: TWIST
### Repeat five times.

Position: same as for previous exercise.

1. Hold hands and raise your child's arms over her head; move her arms so that her upper body twists at the waist.

2. Now twist to the other direction.

# THREE: FALLING LEAVES
Repeat five times.

Position: same as for previous exercise.

1. Hold hands, bringing your child's arms high over her head.

2. Bend forward so your child brings her arms down to the floor. Then slowly come back up to the starting position.

# 10

# The Three- to Five-Year-Olds and Up

# GROUP IV EXERCISES

## *Warm-up*

Purpose: to stretch the body and move the joints, preparing for exercise.

### ONE: ARM SWAY
Repeat eight times.

Position: standing.

1. Reach your arms up over
your head and sway to one
side bending at the waist.
Try not to twist forward or
backward.

2. Now sway to the other
side.

# TWO: CLIMB ROPE
### Repeat ten times.

Position: same as for previous exercise.

1. Reach one arm high over your head. Imagine a string attached to your third finger that pulls you up and stretches your arm as high as it will go. Feel the stretch in your waist as you do this.

2. Now release the first arm and repeat with your other arm.

# THREE: SKIING
## Repeat eight times.

Position: same as for previous exercise.

1. Reach arms high over head.

NOTE: After you and your child can do this well, you can add a deep breathing exercise. Inhale as your arms go up and exhale as they come down.

2. Keeping your arms stretched, bend at the waist and knees sweeping your arms down into a skiing position. Now sweep your arms back up to the starting position.

*113*

## FOUR: RIDING HORSE
One to four minutes.

Position: standing with legs little more than hip distance apart, feet turned out.

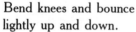
Bend knees and bounce
lightly up and down.

---

# *Aerobics*

---

Purpose: to stimulate heart and lungs (cardiovascular system), building endurance and coordination.

## ONE: JUMPING JACKS
Repeat ten times.

Position: remain standing, facing each other; arms down by sides, feet together parallel.

1. Jump and land with feet a little more than hip distance apart and arms up over your head.

2. Jump again, bringing feet together with arms down at sides.

# TWO: RUNNING IN PLACE
## Two to five minutes.

Position: remain standing facing each other.

1. Run in place with your hands on hips.

2. Continue running and clap hands.

## THREE: LOOKING UNDER THE BRIDGE
Repeat five times.

Position: stand back to back.

1. Bend over keeping legs straight and touching; reach through your legs for each other's hands and hold for the count of five.

2. Release and slowly come up to standing position.

# *Arms*

Purpose: to strengthen the arms, upper body, and waist.

## ONE: HANDS PRESS

Position: stand facing each other.

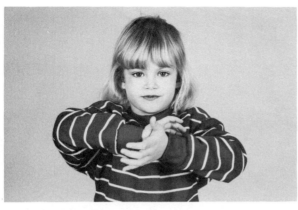

1. Press your own palms together, hands facing in opposite directions.

2. Hold for five seconds, then reverse the position of your hands.

## TWO: WRIST PULL
Repeat three times.

Position: same as for previous exercise.

1. Grasp your wrists and pull; hold for five seconds.

2.  Reverse position of hands and pull for five seconds.

# THREE: TWIST
Repeat five times.

Position: same as for previous exercise.

1.  Hold wrists as in previous exercise; imagine holding a basketball as you twist arms and upper body to one side.

2.  Now twist to the other side.

# FOUR: ARM SCISSORS
Repeat ten times.

Position: same as for previous exercise.

1. Extend your arms in front of you and crisscross arms at wrist.

2. Now crisscross the other way.

# FIVE: FINGER STRETCH AND FISTS

Position: same as for previous exercise.

1. Stretch arms out to the side. Separate and stretch fingers and make small arm circles—forward ten times, then backward ten times.

2. Now make fists and continue arm circles—again, forward ten times, then backward ten times.

## *Torso*

Purpose: to strengthen the abdominal and back muscles, and to stretch the inner thigh and leg muscles.

### ONE: CHURNING
Repeat five times.

Position: sit with your legs apart, your child with her legs apart, touching your legs with her feet.

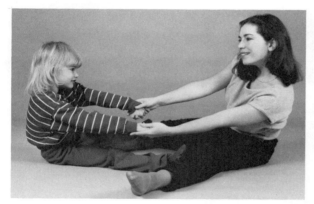

1. Hold hands with arms outstretched and lean to one side.

2. Now lean back.

3. Then lean to other side; then forward.

## TWO: ROWING
Repeat eight times.

Position: same as for previous exercise.

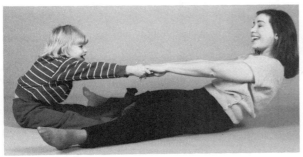

1. Hold hands as before; pull your child forward as you lean backward.

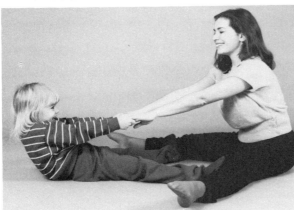

2. Then lean forward, letting your child lean backward.

NOTE: Use your abdominal muscles and feel the muscles in your legs stretch as you do this.

## THREE: SIT-UPS
Repeat five to ten times.

Position: sit with your child between your outstretched legs, facing you.

1. Join hands and lean forward as far as you can, letting your child lean back as far as possible.

2. Now lean back as far as you can, letting your child lean forward.

## FOUR: KNEES UP AND STRETCH
### Repeat five times.

Position: sit side by side, legs outstretched.

1. Lean back with your hands just behind your hips.

2. Bring your knees into your chest.

3. Now straighten your legs, lean over, and reach for your ankles or feet. (Each time you may be able to go a little farther down.) Hold for a few seconds, then slowly come up, returning to the starting position.

## *Legs*

### ONE: HAPPY FEET
Repeat eight times.

Position: sit side by side with your hands behind hips, legs outstretched.

1. Flex your feet hard, bringing your toes up and back toward yourself as far as you can.

2. Now point your toes as far as you can toward the floor.

# TWO: KNEE BEND
### Repeat eight times.

Position: same as for previous exercise.

1. Raise one knee to your chest, keeping the other leg straight.

2. Lower your leg and bring the other knee to your chest.

## THREE: LEG LIFTS
Repeat eight times.

Position: lie on your side facing each other.

1. Raise up on your elbows for support. Lift your upper leg as high as you can, then lower. Repeat eight times.

2. Change sides and repeat eight times with your other leg.

## FOUR: LEG AND BACK STRETCH
Repeat five times.

Position: kneel next to each other on all fours.

1. Lift one leg in the air behind you as you arch your back and look up.

2. Now lower the leg and raise your other leg.

## FIVE: BRIDGE
Repeat five times.

Position: lie side by side, knees bent, feet on the floor.

1. Lift your torso as high as you can, making a bridge with your body.

2. Lower your torso, knees bent.

> NOTE: Be sure to make your leg and buttocks muscles work as you do this to get the maximum benefit from the exercise.

## SIX: FOLDING STRETCH
One time.

Position: kneel on the floor.

1. Bend forward, bringing your torso over your legs, arms outstretched.

2. Hold as long as you like.

> NOTE: This exercise stretches the muscles used in the previous exercise.

# Back

Purpose: to strengthen and relax the back.

## ONE: WILLOW TREE
### Repeat five times.

Position: sit with your legs apart, your child with her legs apart, touching your legs with her feet.

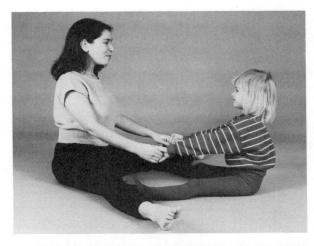

1. Join hands. Lower one arm and raise the other as you bend over your lowered arm.

2. Come up and bend to the other side.

## TWO: KNEE KISS
### Repeat five times.

Position: same as previous exercise.

1. Stretch both your arms over one leg, coming down as far as you can toward your knee. You may eventually be able to kiss your knee.

2. Now reach over to the other knee and lean down.

# THREE: HEAD ROLL
### Repeat five times.

Position: same as previous exercise.

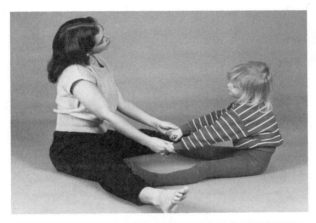

1. Join hands, sitting up straight. Roll your head to one side.

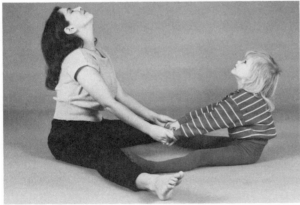

2. Now continue rolling your head back.

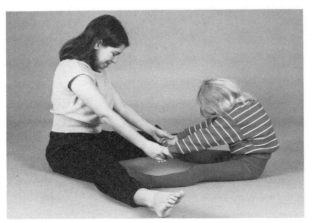

3. Continue rolling your head to the other side, then forward.

# III

# Massage Program

# 11

# Getting Ready for Massage

Before you begin to massage your baby or child there are a few things you can do to make this a safe and enjoyable activity. As with the exercise program, you won't need a large area or any special equipment. The most comfortable place for the massage will depend on you and your child. You may find that at bedtime the bed will be the best place, since your child or baby may fall asleep during the massage. At other times, you may want to massage on the floor or sitting in a large chair.

When the weather is nice, massaging out of doors will be both relaxing and pleasurable. Whether you are indoors or out, be sure that there are no drafts. Nothing ruins a massage more than being cold. If it is very hot or if the sun is quite strong, find some shade to protect you and your child or baby.

You can either massage the baby on your lap or on a padded surface; a bed, blanket, or towel will do. I suggest trying both to find which is best for you. I have found that babies and children alike enjoy having a sheepskin under them. With the fuzzy side up, this provides children with a cuddly texture under them that is both warm and comforting. I use a small carpet that has goat's hair on one side and smooth wool on the other side. If you have one or something like it, you may want to use it. A towel, blanket, or pad with some texture to it will provide your baby with additional tactile stimulation.

It is important that you also be comfortable. Make sure that you have back support in the form of a pillow, wall, or chairback. Otherwise, sit in a manner that is most comfortable. Take off your rings and any other jewelry that would get in the way. Fingernails should be trimmed so as not to scratch your child.

Your baby can either be diapered or nude. If you massage your baby nude, be prepared for him to relax in more ways than one! It might be wise to have a diaper or towel handy just in case. Your older child might also go without clothes or wear underwear or a bathing suit.

If you would like to use oil for the massage, have some cold-pressed vegetable oil on hand or use a baby lotion. I find that baby oil is too thin to use.

Now that you are ready to begin massage, hug your baby or child and tell him what you are going to do. Make the environment as pleasing as possible. This will help you both to look forward to massage each day. Have some toys or a pacifier on hand for your baby to hold while you massage him or her. (You don't have to use these.) You may want to play some relaxing music.

If you are using oil or lotion, take a few drops in your hand and rub your hands together. Then smooth the oil over the area you are going to massage.

Massage actually involves a number of different strokes, which differ according to the amount of pressure used. The lightest form of massage is called "effleurage." This involves very light stroking of the skin. In this book, effleurage will be referred to as light stroking. Medium pressure and deep pressure strokes are used to work into the muscles. With medium pressure, you should see a slight indentation in the skin. If you press a little harder, you will be using deep pressure strokes. The massage instruction gives guidelines as to which strokes to use.

If your baby gets restless during the massage, feel free to take a feeding break and either resume the massage afterward or come back to it at another time. You may also want to stop to take a "cuddle break" during the massage.

Touch communicates feelings better than words can. Therefore, it is important that you not massage your baby or child if you are distressed or not feeling well. Your baby would probably sense this and the massage would not be a pleasant one for him.

As your child gets a little older, the massage routine will differ only slightly from the one you used with your baby. You will be massaging with a little more pressure than before. Additionally, you will be helping your child get over his growing pains and easing his sore muscles at times.

Your older child may also be happy to use what he has learned from you giving him massage. Children enjoy giving massages to their parents. It gives them a sense of pride knowing that they can do something for their parents that they will appreciate. The father and son who were photographed for this book are now exchanging massages regularly. Nicholas also now massages his mother's shoulders when she asks him to.

Siblings can be given massages by older brothers and sisters with parental supervision. Wait until the baby is at least a year old before allowing an older sibling to massage him. Make sure your child understands the importance of being gentle and that you watch closely while one child massages the other.

Like the exercise program, the massage program can go with you wherever you go. You can use it whenever you like. Use massage at bedtime to help your child or baby get to sleep. Use it when your child is cranky. Massage will come as a welcome relief for your older child who is suffering growing pains. It will help your older child feel more at ease with himself. Massage can be used after exercising. It can be used to help your sleepy child get up in the morning.

Above all, massage will bring you and your child closer. It will help you feel comfortable with each other. It will give your child a feeling of security and comfort. Very soon you, too, might receive a massage from your child! Until then, you and your spouse can use the same massage methods to help each other relax.

A few final points before starting to massage:

- You can use the strokes described in the following chapters for children of any age as well as for adults.
- With your baby, you might begin by massaging a few minutes a day, gradually building up to about thirty minutes a day. Some parents massage their children twice a day.
- As in the case of exercise, massage should never be forced on a child.

# 12

# Massage Program
# for the First Two Years

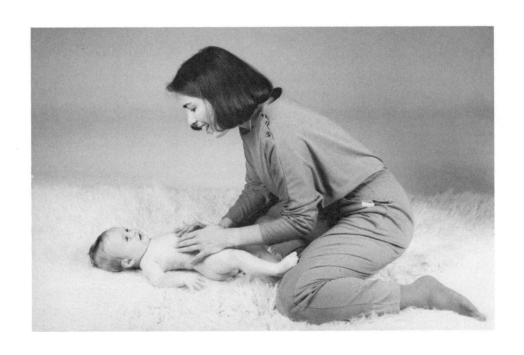

## *Relaxation Hold—Light Pressure*

Position: your baby lies on your outstretched legs or in front of you on a blanket, bed, or other firm padded surface.

Place your hands lightly over your baby's ears, fingers curved around the back of your baby's head. Thumbs are on your baby's cheeks. Hold for a minute or longer, or as long as your baby responds and enjoys.

## *Face—Light Pressure*

Massage the face using tiny circular strokes. Massage the forehead from the center to the sides, the cheeks, the jaw, and lightly in small circles around the eyes.

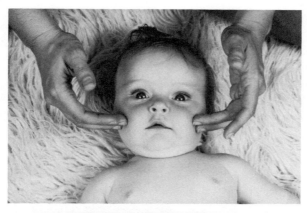

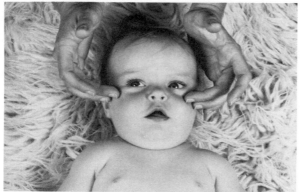

## Head—Light Pressure

Using the fingertips of both hands, lightly stroke your baby's head with tiny circular strokes. Begin at the crown and massage all parts of the head.

## Neck—Medium Pressure

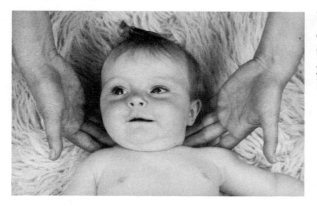

With the thumbs and fingers of both hands, gently stroke the muscles on either side of your baby's neck from the base to the top of the neck.

## Shoulders—Medium Pressure

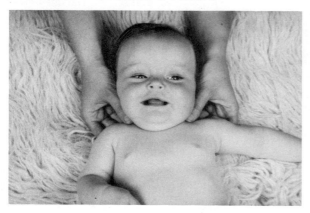

Use thumbs and fingers to gently squeeze the muscles in the shoulders from the base of the neck to the shoulder joint.

## *Arms and Hands—Medium Pressure*

1. Take baby's hand in one hand. Using both hands, begin massaging with your thumbs and fingers from the shoulder to the wrist. Squeeze lightly into the large muscles in the upper and lower arm. Repeat with other arm.

2. Using your thumbs and fingers, massage the palm and outside of your baby's hand using tiny circular strokes.

3. Now gently stroke each tiny finger from the base to the tip. Use your thumb and first two fingers to do this. Repeat with the other hand.

NOTE: Do not pull on the arm.

## Chest—Medium Pressure

Using your fingers, stroke from the center of the chest to the sides, working from top of chest to bottom of rib cage. Repeat many times.

## Stomach—Medium Pressure

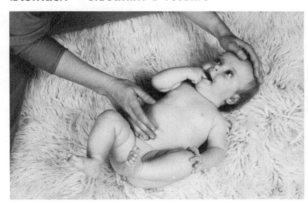

1. Place the balls of the fingers of one hand at the lower right side of your baby's stomach. Rest your other hand on her head. Using a little pressure, move your fingers in a clockwise pattern around the stomach. Complete the circle three to five times.

2. Using fingertips in circular strokes, massage around the navel. Use medium pressure as you massage in a clockwise pattern. Use only after two months of age.

## Legs—Medium Pressure

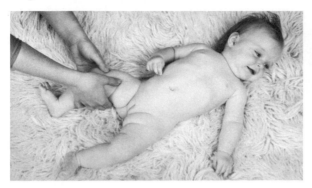

Take baby's leg and beginning at the thigh, massage down to the ankle, squeezing with your fingers and thumbs as you go. Use your thumbs to massage into the large muscles of the legs.

## Feet—Medium Pressure

Position: as before except that your baby's feet now point toward you rather than away from you.

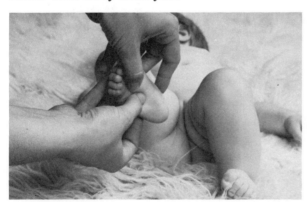

1. Gently using your thumbs, massage the soles of each foot with small circular strokes.

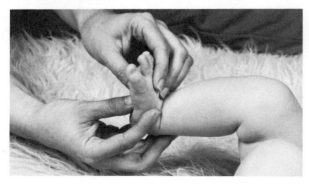

2. At the same time, using your fingers of both hands, lightly stroke the top of each foot.

3. Using your thumb and first two fingers, gently stroke each toe. Stroke from the base to the tip of each toe.

## Front Strokes—Light Pressure

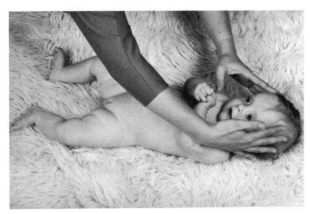

1. Begin with your fingertips touching at the crown and covering your baby's head.

2. Using very light pressure, stroke down your baby's head and neck to the shoulders. Continue the stroke over the chest, torso, hips, and legs to the toes. When you come to the toes, brush off as though brushing dust off the feet.

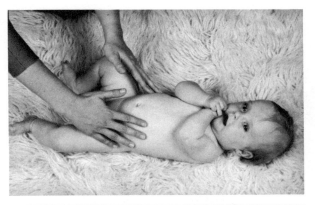

NOTE: Repeat five times or as long as your baby enjoys.

## *Back of Shoulders—Medium Pressure*

Position: baby on stomach.

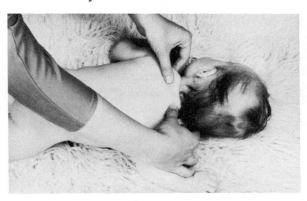

Using your thumbs and fingers, gently squeeze the shoulder ridge, massaging from the base of the neck to the outer part of the shoulders.

## Back—Medium Pressure

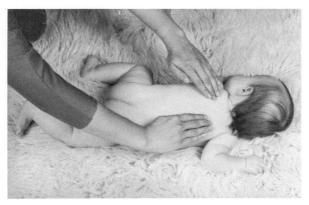

1. With your hands on either side of the spine, stroke up and down your baby's back using small short movements of your hands.

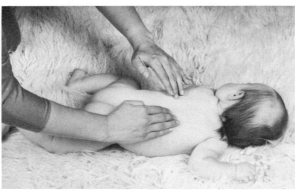

2. Use the balls of your fingers to massage the back from the shoulders to the buttocks with small circular strokes.

> NOTE: Never massage directly over the spine or use any pressure on the spine itself.

## Buttocks—Medium Pressure

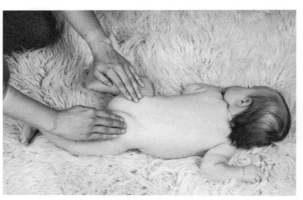

Using the balls of your fingers, massage in tiny circles all over the buttocks. Use enough pressure to work into the large muscles of the buttocks. Use firm but gentle strokes.

## *Back of the Legs—Medium Pressure*

Position: your baby lies on his stomach on your outstretched legs or on a padded surface, feet pointing toward you.

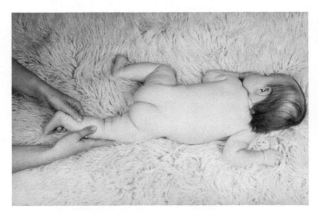

Beginning at the top of the thigh, use both hands as you squeeze from the top of the thigh down to the ankle. As you squeeze, use your thumbs to gently but firmly massage into the large muscular parts of the thigh and calf.

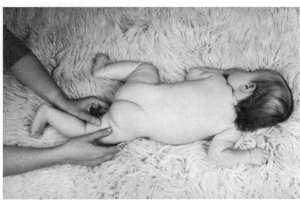

## *Back Strokes—Light Pressure*

1. Begin with hands together, fingers pointing upward at the crown of the head.

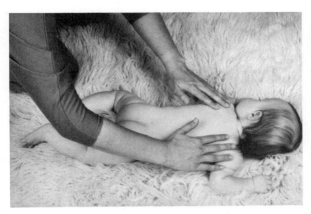

2. Move down the neck over the shoulders down the back, buttocks, and legs to the feet. Brush off at the feet with a light, feathery stroke.

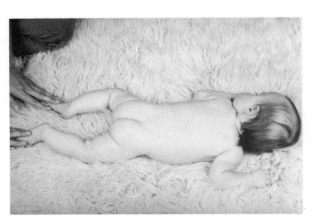

## *Ending Relaxation Holds—Light Pressure (I)*

Position: baby on stomach.

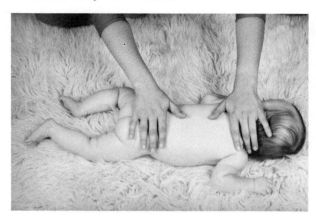

Place your right hand over the low back and your left hand curved gently around the neck. Hold very lightly as long as your baby enjoys it or until she falls asleep.

## *Ending Relaxation Holds—Light Pressure (II)*

Position: baby on her back.

Place your left hand over your baby's forehead, palm over the center, fingers curved around her head. Place your right palm over the navel. Hold very lightly for as long as your baby enjoys or until she falls asleep.

# 13

# Massage Program
# for Age Two and Up

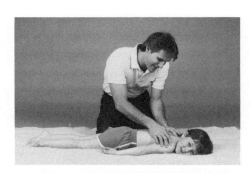

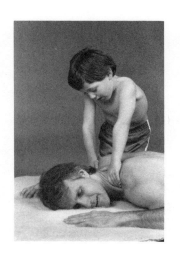

## *Relaxation Holds—Light Pressure*

Position: your child is lying on his back.

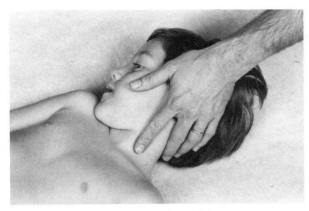

1. Place both hands over your child's ears with thumbs along the jaw and fingers curved under the neck. Hold very lightly for a minute or longer.

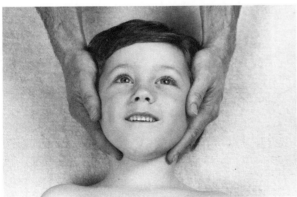

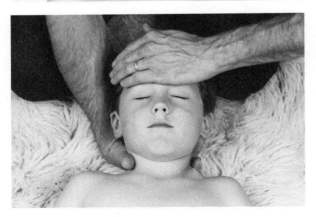

2. Place one hand over the child's forehead and the other under the neck; palm is at the base of the neck with fingers curving around the neck. Hold for a minute or longer.

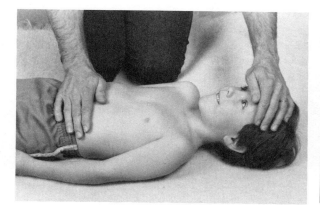

3. Place one hand across the forehead as before and the other palm over the navel and fingers on the stomach. Hold for a minute or longer.

4. Now you may rock both hands very lightly.

NOTE: Find which hold your child responds to best. It may be different each time.

## Face—Light Pressure

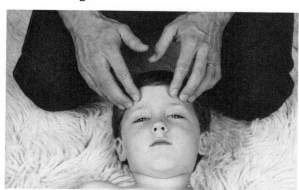

1. Using your fingers, massage the forehead with tiny circular strokes. Begin at the center of the forehead moving to the sides of the face.

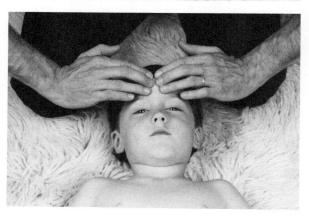

2. Using your fingertips, stroke from the center of the forehead to the sides.

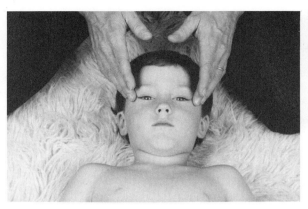

3. Using your third or second finger, circle the eyes from the corners down, then up and back to the corners.

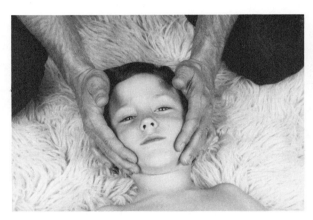

4. Using your fingers, stroke from the tip of the chin along the jaw to the temple. At the temple, use tiny, feather-light circular strokes.

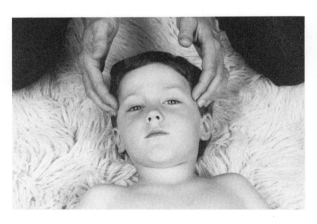

5. Using your fingers, massage the rest of the face with tiny circular strokes.

## *Head—Medium or Light Pressure*

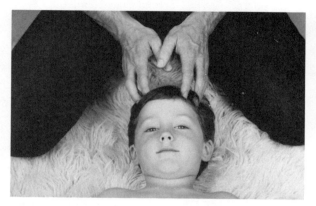

Using fingertips, massage the entire head with tiny circular strokes. Use light pressure if your child is about to go to sleep or if you are quieting the child. Use slightly more pressure at other times.

## *Neck—Medium Pressure*

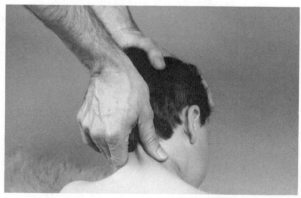

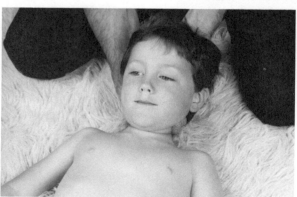

1. Cup the head in one hand. With the thumbs and fingers of the other hand, gently squeeze the muscles on either side of the neck from the base to the top of the neck.

2. Turn the head to one side and cup in your hand. With the fingers of your other hand lightly massage the neck from the base to the top using tiny circular strokes. Repeat on the other side of the neck.

## *Shoulders—Medium to Deep Pressure*

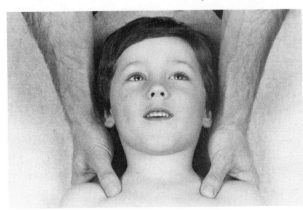

Use thumbs and fingers to gently squeeze muscles in the shoulders from the base of the neck to the shoulder joints.

## Arms and Hands—Medium to Deep Pressure

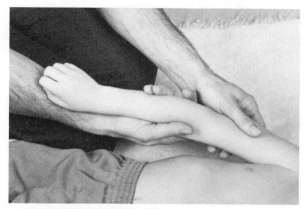

1. Using medium pressure, gently squeeze the arm with your hands as you work from the shoulder to the wrist. Use your thumbs to work into the larger muscles of the arms. Repeat with the child's other arm.

2. Using your thumbs, massage the palms of the hands with small circular strokes. At the same time, massage the tops of the hands with your fingers.

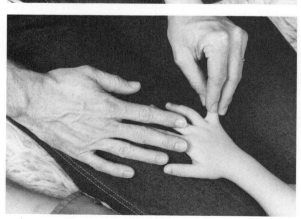

3. With the thumb and first two fingers of one hand, stroke each of your child's fingers from the base to the tip, holding your child's hand in your other hand. Repeat on the fingers of the other hand.

## Chest—Medium to Deep Pressure

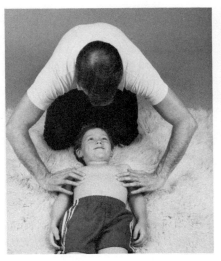

Using your fingers, massage the chest beginning at the center or sternum and working out to the sides of the chest. Use long, even strokes and repeat five to ten times.

## Stomach—Medium Pressure

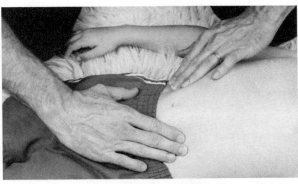

1. Massage the stomach in a circular pattern, moving your hands clockwise from the lower right side of the child's stomach, up to the beginning of the rib cage, then across the stomach, down along the left side and to the lower right side of stomach.

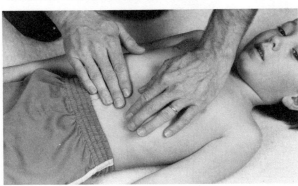

2. Using the balls of your fingers, massage the center of the stomach over the navel in circular clockwise strokes.

## Legs—Medium to Deep Pressure

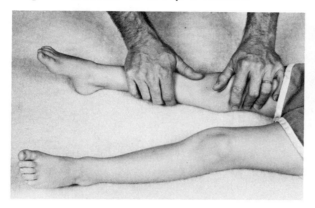

1. Beginning at the thigh, massage down to the ankle, squeezing with your fingers and thumbs. Use your thumbs to work into the larger muscles of the legs.

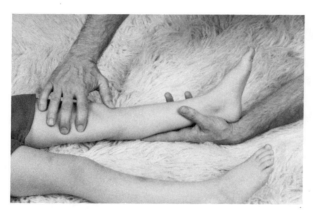

2. Holding the leg in one hand, massage with the other hand, using your fingertips in small circular strokes over the entire leg.

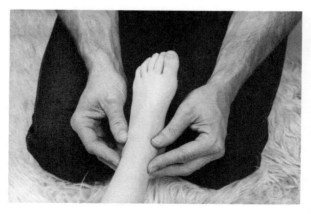

3. Massage around the anklebone and in back and front of the ankle.

## *Feet—Medium to Deep Pressure*

1. Using your thumbs in small circular strokes, gently work into the soles of your child's feet.

2. Using your fingers, lightly massage the top of the feet with small circular strokes.

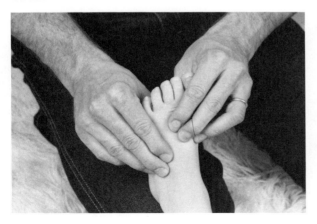

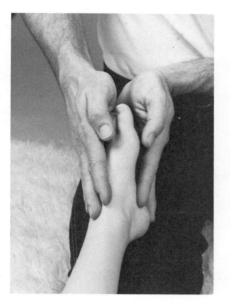 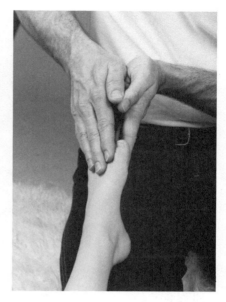

3. With the fingers of one hand on top of the ankle and the fingers of the other hand on your child's heel, gently brush each foot with your fingers from the heel and ankle to the toes. Repeat this as many times as your child likes.

## Front Strokes—Light Pressure

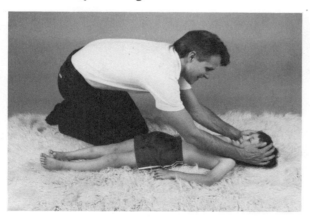

1. Begin with your fingers on your child's head.

2. Using very light pressure, stroke down your child's head, neck, shoulders, and continue to stroke over the chest, torso, hips, and legs to the toes. Begin again at the head and repeat.

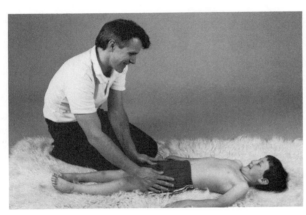

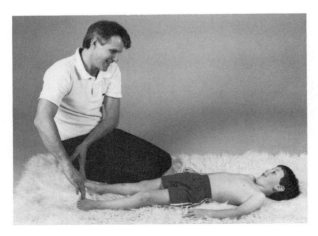

## Back of the Neck—Light to Medium Pressure

Position: your child lies on his stomach on a padded surface.

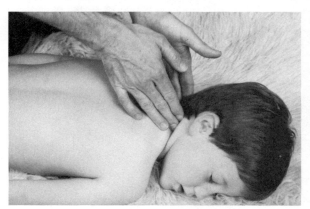

Beginning at the top of the neck, use your second and third fingers in very tiny circular strokes to either side of the spine down to the base of the neck. Repeat two to five times.

## Shoulders—Medium to Deep Pressure

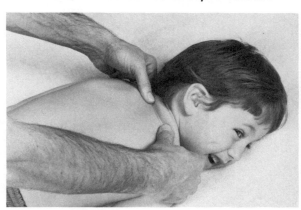

Using your thumbs and fingers, gently squeeze the shoulder ridge, massaging from the base of the neck to the shoulder joints. As you squeeze the muscle, pull toward you.

## *Back—Medium Pressure*

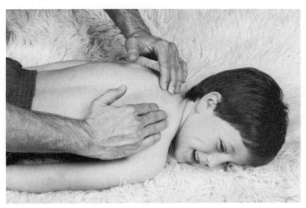

1. Using the balls of your fingers, massage the entire back with small circular strokes. *Do not massage directly on the spine.*

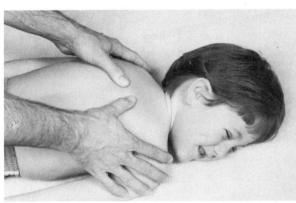

2. Using thumbs, press gently but firmly to either side of the spine at the base of the neck. Release, and press again slightly lower than previously. Continue pressing points to either side of the spine until you come to the lower back. Press lightly in the lower part of the back using very little pressure. Repeat one to three times.

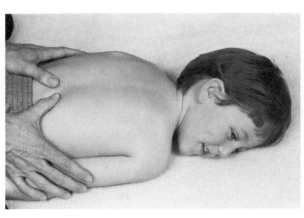

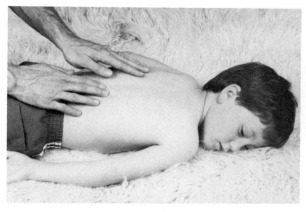

3. Using your palms, massage each side of the back from the shoulders to the buttocks, hands parallel to the spine. Use very light pressure in the lower part of the back and never use any pressure directly on the spine.

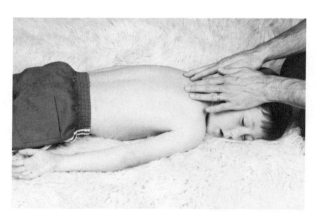

4. Beginning at the shoulders, stroke down the back to either side of the spine using both hands.

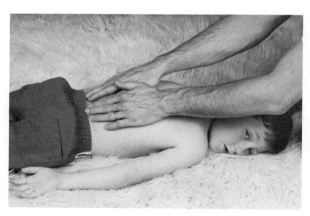

5. When you reach the lower back, begin stroking up the back, fingers pointing down. Stroke up the sides of the back.

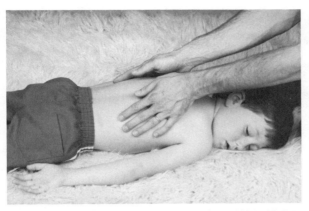

6. When you reach the shoulders, indent the muscles with your hands, coming close to the spine again.

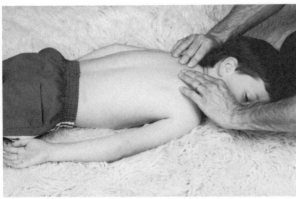

7. Massage the shoulders, squeezing with your fingers and thumbs from the base of the neck to the shoulder joint. Repeat the entire sequence.

## *Back of the Legs—Medium to Deep Pressure*

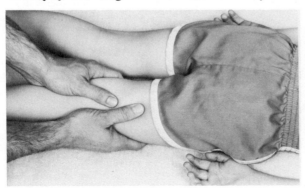

1. Beginning at the top of the thigh, use both hands as you squeeze from the top of the thigh down to the ankle. As you squeeze, use your thumbs to work into the large muscular parts of the thigh and calf.

2. Using fingers, begin at the buttocks and lightly stroke the entire length of the leg to the foot. Repeat two to five times with each leg.

## Back Strokes—Light Pressure

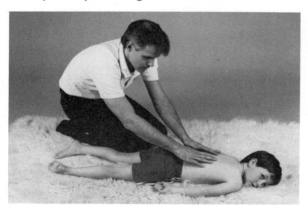

1. Begin with hands together placed lightly on the head.

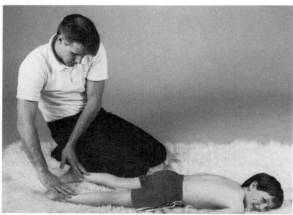

2. Lightly stroke down the neck, over the shoulders, and down the back, buttocks, and legs to the feet. Brush off at the feet and repeat.

## *Ending Relaxation Holds—Light Pressure*

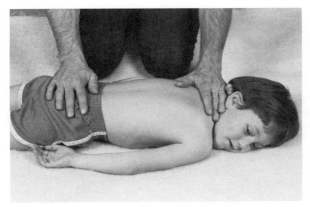

1. Place your right hand lightly over the coccyx and your left hand lightly over and curved around the neck. Hold for a few seconds.

   Keeping your left hand over the neck, move your right hand over the middle of the back. Hold for a few seconds, return to the original position, and hold for a few seconds.

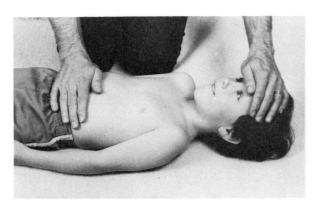

2. Your child lies on his back again. Place your right hand over his navel, left hand over the forehead. Use light pressure and hold for a few seconds or as long as your child enjoys this.

# 14

# Conclusion

Presented in this book are invaluable tools and information for parents and children. Used judiciously with respect for a child's individual needs and temperament, they may augment his overall development and enhance the bond of love between parent and child.

In using this book, parents will find answers to many questions regarding child rearing. For instance, fathers have long been ignored for their contributions as care givers and nurturers. In reading and using this book, they will find a unique avenue for deep involvement with their children from infancy onward. The exercise and massage programs provide fathers with an opportunity to strengthen the growing bond between them.

Mothers will also find these programs helpful in bonding with their children. Eye contact, verbal communication, and especially touching are known to be important factors in the bonding process. The massage and exercise programs demonstrated in this book provide for ample use of all of these stimuli.

While tending to the need for parental-child bonding, these programs also do much to relieve stress. Stress has only recently been found to afflict children as well as adults. The effects of cumulative stress are as disastrous for children as for their parents. Along with reducing stress, the massage and exercise programs teach children invaluable lessons for coping with stress throughout life.

Most important, in embarking on the massage and exercise routines, parents and children stand to gain immeasurably from the hours of enjoyment spent together. It is with this sentiment that I urge you to begin massaging and exercising with your children!

# INDEX

# Index